D0061587

"This timely and outstanding book demonstrates the many predatory ways that debt stifles mobility for the most economically vulnerable. Fortunately it does not conclude there but presents a political pathway. Through solidarity and collective action, debtors' unions can forge a new economy that prioritizes finance working for all people, rather than our most vulnerable working for finance."

—Darrick Hamilton

"This book explains why we are overdue for a debt revolution and, more importantly, how to do it. To abolish debt is to begin to rebuild society. We need to start doing so now."

—David Graeber

"*Can't Pay, Won't Pay* is a clear, readable, and hugely powerful account of debt resistance in the age of financialized capitalism. Debt Collective brilliantly summarizes the contradictions of debt-fueled growth, and demonstrates how ordinary people can work together to resist it. *Can't Pay, Won't Pay* is the bible of debt resistance—a must-read for activists and academics alike."

—Grace Blakeley

CAN'T ~~PAY~~ WON'T ~~PAY~~

THE CASE FOR
ECONOMIC DISOBEDIENCE
AND DEBT ABOLITION

 HAYMARKET BOOKS | CHICAGO, ILLINOIS

Published in 2020 by
Haymarket Books
P.O. Box 180165
Chicago, IL 60618
773-583-7884
www.haymarketbooks.org
info@haymarketbooks.org

ISBN: 978-1-64259-262-7

Distributed to the trade in the US through Consortium
Book Sales and Distribution (www.cbsd.com)
and internationally through Ingram Publisher Services
International (www.ingramcontent.com).

This book was published with the generous support
of Lannan Foundation and Wallace Action Fund.

Cover design by Chase Whiteside.
Graphics by Jared Bajkowski.

Library of Congress Cataloging-in-Publication
data is available.

Printed in Canada by union labor.

10 9 8 7 6 5 4 3 2 1

CONTENTS

FOREWORD

I n 2008, around the same time Lehman Brothers collapsed and the mortgage market began to melt down, I got a call telling me my student loans were in default. I remember trying to grasp the logic as I spoke to the collector. Because I didn't have money, they were increasing my principal by 19 percent. My balance ballooned, as did my monthly payments, which meant I was even more broke than before. My credit score tanked, further compounding my financial woes.

When I got involved in Occupy Wall Street a few years later, I realized my situation was hardly unique. Most people drawn to the encampments were also in the red. To talk to fellow protesters during the first few weeks of Occupy Wall Street was to talk about student loans that couldn't be repaid, medical bills that were piling up, houses that had been foreclosed on by bailed-out banks, and insolvent communities forced to endure austerity measures, with people of color hit hardest. Millions were homeless and jobless, delaying starting families or losing hope of ever being able to retire, while bankers got massive bonuses. Perhaps organizing around in-debtedness, some of us thought, would be worthwhile.

That's what those of us who wrote this book have been working to do ever since. What follows is a jointly authored record of insights and ideas developed over years with various collaborators too numerous to name individually. Our efforts kicked off in April 2012 when the Occupy Student Debt Campaign (OSDC) organized a protest marking "1T Day"—the day outstanding student debt hit one trillion dollars—and demanding full debt cancellation and free public college. (The 1T protest was the first time I ever heard anyone make the call for student debt cancellation, and I was enrapt). Over the coming months, OSDC merged forces with Strike Debt, a decentralized initiative focused primarily on public education. Strike Debt hosted debtors' assemblies, where strangers gathered and shared personal stories, and collaborated on a pamphlet called the *Debt Resisters' Operations Manual*, which combined practical financial advice and a radical overview of our economic system. A little over a year after Occupy began, we launched the Rolling Jubilee, a crowd-funded project that erased more than $30 million of medical, tuition, payday loan, and criminal punishment debt belonging to thousands of strangers. We acted just like debt collectors, buying port-folios of debt on shadowy secondary debt markets for pen-nies on the dollar, but instead of collecting on them we erased them, sending people letters notifying them that their obli-gations were gone, no strings attached. In 2014 we formally launched the Debt Collective, a union for debtors.

Over the years we have developed a shared understanding of the central role debt plays in our economy and the
way debt might be wielded as a form of power, an analysis
we share in the following pages. Debt, we realized, bridges
the individual and the structural, the personal and political,
binding each of us to a broader set of financial and political
circumstances—circumstances that have emerged over centuries of racist, colonialist, and capitalist exploitation and
wealth accumulation. Our goal has been to devise new creative ways to organize. Specifically, turning our individual
indebtedness into a source of collective leverage in order to
transform those broader conditions. As Marx famously said,
the point isn't just to interpret the world but to change it.

Taking inspiration from the labor movement, we believe
debtors organized in a union can exercise material power over
their common circumstances. The two modes of organizing
have different targets but complementary aims. Where labor
unions focus on sites of production, debtors' unions focus
on circulation, or how money and capital flow and to whom.
Labor organizing targets the employer, demanding higher
wages, benefits, and more. Debtor organizing, on the other
hand, targets the creditor (which, in the era of neoliberalism is also often the state). Debtor organizing fights *against*
predatory financial contracts and *for* the universal provision
of public goods, including healthcare, education, housing,
and retirement, so that people don't have to go into debt to
access them. These public goods and their access must be
structured in ways that remedy long-standing and ongoing

social inequalities. The Debt Collective believes that it is not enough for public goods and social services to be universal, they must be *reparative*, too.

One of the upsides to debtor organizing is that, unlike worker organizing, there have not been decades of class war aimed to suppress the tactic. Since the Labor Management Relations Act, typically known as Taft-Hartley, was passed in 1947, a lot of seemingly sensible union organizing strategies are simply illegal. The war on labor unions helps explain why only a small percentage of workers are organized on the job (about 6 percent in the private sector and 30 percent in the public sector). The core activities of organizing debtors have not been overtly regulated or restricted in the same way, leaving room to experiment. Debtor organizing has the potential to bring millions of people who may never have the option of joining a traditional labor union into the struggle for economic justice.

What follows is a document of collective thinking and an invitation to collective action. Like employers, creditors have enormous power over people's lives. We are forced to debt-finance healthcare, education, housing, and even our own incarceration. When we can't pay, debtors are disciplined with steep penalties, high interest rates or loan denials, and damaged credit scores, not to mention poverty, as unpayable bills come due. State power is often deployed to enforce unfair financial contracts through court judgments, garnishments, and even jail time. This book does not advise financial suicide but coordinated and strategic campaigns of resistance. An individual default is not a debt strike. As with any organizing campaign, there is no guarantee of success. Bosses retaliate against workers, and creditors can be expected to do the same to debtors who dare to throw down the gauntlet. But it is worth the risk, because the present is unbearable. Although many older people are also deeply indebted, the rising generation is the first in a century to face more dismal economic prospects than their parents, in part because they are being crushed by debt. In the United States, for example, student debt now surpasses $1.7 trillion. In better news, that's $1.7 trillion of leverage to use in the fight for a different economic system.

If we don't get organized, debtors will keep getting pushed deeper into a financial hole. In the throes of the pandemic, some payday lenders are charging close to 800 percent interest on short-term loans, taking advantage of people who have no other way to keep a roof over their heads or put food on the table. Mass unemployment in the absence of a functioning safety net intensifies mass indebtedness, fueling the already vastly unequal distribution of wealth along predictable racial lines. Meanwhile, financiers are becoming more powerful. When the stock market tanked, the Trump administration put the world's largest asset manager, BlackRock, in charge of a multitrillion-dollar federal fund tasked with buying up corporate debt. Yet the tens of millions of people who lost their jobs are expected to continue making monthly payments to banks and bill collectors.

We've entered unprecedented territory, but we're not powerless. Over the last decade, once fringe left-wing ideas have become mainstream. Free higher education, universal health care, a Green New Deal, defunding and abolishing the police, and debt cancellation are now popular policies, thanks to grassroots pressure. I'll never forget how, back in 2012, 1T Day organizers were met with derision from the mainstream press when they called for student debt relief and free college. "They want all student debt in the country forgiven. All $1 trillion of it. And if the government would be so kind, they'd appreciate it if it would pay for higher education from here on out, as well," Reuters' Chadwick Matlin snarked. "What has happened to this proposal? Hardly anybody has cared." NPR's *All Things Considered* also covered the action, reporting that "most experts believe there's little chance the government would ever forgive student loans." Those so-called experts were dead wrong. Over the last five years Debt Collective members succeeded in forcing the government to cancel more than a billion dollars' worth of student loans and put student debt at the center of the 2020 presidential primary cycle.

The moral of the story is that we have to keep organizing. If we don't, the crisis of indebtedness will only become more acute in the years to come. Personal debt has reached historic proportions, totaling $14 trillion, and staggering rates of unemployment and a decimated social safety net only raise the stakes. The chant that rang out at Occupy—"Banks got bailed out, we got sold out"—resonates in 2020, only it wasn't just the banks that got a lifeline when COVID-19 crashed the economy. The cruise and hotel industries, the fossil fuel sector, meat packing plants, private equity firms, and more all lined up to receive public money while regular people were hung out to dry.

We need an organized, militant debtors' movement now more than ever. Given the way capitalism isolates and divides us, we have long needed to find a way to organize across physical distance and social difference, and debtors' unions offer one promising approach. Debtors who share common creditors are rarely confined to a single geographical location. Unlike workers, debtors don't share a factory floor or office but are connected nevertheless, bound by the same creditors and an economic system that forces them into debt for basic needs. Coordinated campaigns of debt renegotiation and refusal can include people who live on opposite sides of the country, opposite ends of the city, or, in some cases, on the other side of the world.

I write this in the midst of intersecting crises. A public health crisis coupled with an economic crisis have intensified and exposed longstanding racial inequities, catalyzing a global movement against police brutality and white supremacy. With huge numbers of people newly out of work and vital social services being slashed, one thing is certain: many households, disproportionately households of color, will be forced to take on massive debts to survive the next year. Life was already difficult before COVID-19 crashed the economy; things are now becoming untenable. Racial capitalism is a centuries-long pandemic. We cannot afford not to rebel.

These days, the words *crisis* and *apocalyptic* couldn't be more apt. The first term comes from the Ancient Greek and means the turning point in an illness—death or recovery, two stark alternatives. The root of *apocalypse* means to reveal or uncover. This is the truth unveiled by this apocalyptic moment: to truly cure ourselves and survive this crisis we are going to need way more than a vaccine. We will also need more than debt write-downs or even debt abolition to heal what ails us, though that would be a welcome start. We need to completely transform our economy and society so that millions of people don't have to live in perpetual financial and physical peril. We offer our thinking, research, and proposals as a resource for everyone struggling to build a better world.

—Astra Taylor, June 2020

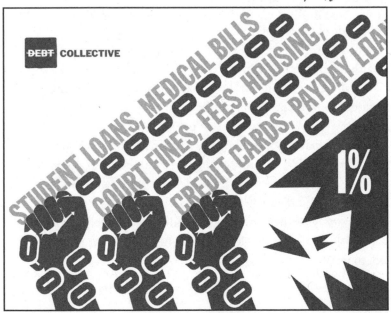

INTRODUCTION

WE OWN THE BANK

I n early 2020 Pam Hunt got an email letting her know that the approximately $40,000 in student loans she incurred for attending a for-profit college would be erased by the US Department of Education. The Trump administration did not make the decision to cancel Pam's debt as an act of kindness—far from it. Officials were forced to act because debtors had been engaged in a years-long campaign of economic disobedience. Trump's billionaire secretary of education, Betsy DeVos, only issued discharges with what she described as "extreme displeasure."

In 2015, in partnership with the Debt Collective, fifteen former students of a predatory, for-profit college chain called Corinthian launched the first student debt strike in history. Hundreds and then thousands joined the movement. Strikers were young, old, Black, white, gay, straight; they lived in urban centers and rural communities. What they had in common was debt. Everyone had attended a criminal, for-profit college that had systematically defrauded its students, burying them in unpayable loans while funneling money to shareholders. The Corinthian strikers argued that their debts were illegitimate and should be canceled. For-profit colleges, they insisted, should be shut down and public education made free for all.

If you are reading this, there's a chance you can relate to the student debt strikers, even if you didn't attend a for-profit college. Maybe you also borrowed money to attend school or have other bills you struggle to pay. You can probably imagine the feeling of relief that would come if your debts were abolished. Most of us have debt of some kind, whether it's student loans, housing debt, credit card debt, medical debt, utility bills, court fines and fees, or payday loans. As was the case for Pam—a single mother and cancer survivor whose student debt load made it difficult for her to find secure housing—debt compounds our other problems. The weight of our debt pulls us all down, though the chains of compound interest tug more heavily on some than others. A 2016 study found that Black graduates have about $7,400 more in student debt than their white counterparts upon graduation; four years after leaving college, that gap has increased to $25,000. A combination of predatory interest rates and discriminatory low wages (earning less makes it harder to pay back a loan) ensure that Black women like Pam suffer the most. Black women have the highest student debt burdens, which means they end up paying more for the same educational experience as their often wealthier white counterparts.

All told, more than one million student debtors default every year. But what if, instead of drowning alone, people engaged in collective refusal? That's what happened during the debt strike. People who didn't know each other banded together and realized that their debts don't have to be a shameful burden—they can become a form of leverage. The fact that Pam—along with tens of thousands of other people—got her student loans canceled proves as much.

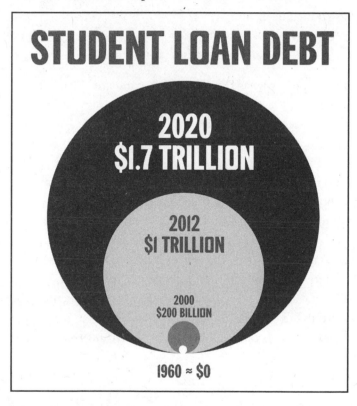

STUDENT LOAN DEBT

2020
$1.7 TRILLION

2012
$1 TRILLION

2000
$200 BILLION

1960 ≈ $0

To conduct the kind of mass politics that can succeed at scale, debtors need an institutional base. We need debtors' unions: associations of indebted people and their allies, who are willing to engage in campaigns of economic disobedience and threaten collective nonpayment. Debtors' unions can harness the power of debt and wield it strategically. Individually, our debts overwhelm us. But together they make us powerful. Creditors are already organized—that's why they got bailed out in 2008 and 2020 and have more influence over our lives than ever before. The time has come for debtors to get organized, too.

IN THE RED

In early 2020, when the COVID-19 pandemic first began to destabilize the global economy, eighty-seven million US residents lacked adequate healthcare coverage and 40 percent could not afford an unexpected four-hundred-dollar expense.

The pandemic created a crisis; it also revealed one. In the richest country in the history of the world, forty million people were poor (including more than 40 percent of all children), half of all workers lived paycheck to paycheck, and 12 percent of the population had experienced food insecurity at some point during the preceding year. Nearly one in five renters could not pay their rent for part of 2017. When the Coronavirus hit, things went from bad to worse. People who were already struggling suddenly had no way to make ends meet. The virus was a double threat, something that could be a death sentence or lead to financial ruin. With no savings to fall back on, people were driven deeper into debt and default.

The danger posed wasn't equally distributed. The disease affected communities according to predictable lines of class, race, and ability. In places like Detroit, Milwaukee, New Orleans, and Chicago, as well as in the Bronx and Queens, Black people were hit particularly hard by the virus. More likely to be employed in "essential" industries, many lacked the privilege to work from home, which increased their risk of exposure. To make matters worse, poor people suffer disproportionately from conditions such as heart disease and diabetes, underlying illnesses that increase the risk of dying from the virus.

Just as the virus ravages those with underlying conditions, this book aims to provide an analysis of economic conditions that made millions of people so financially vulnerable when the outbreak happened. We live in a world where a handful of billionaires (soon to be trillionaires) control more wealth than half of humanity. Their fortunes grow at our expense, the lucky few raking in unearned income and dividends while the majority of people can barely stay afloat. The ruling class's relentless attacks on organized labor and refusal to pay taxes meant there was no safety net to catch regular people when the economy collapsed.

For decades, taking on debt has been the only solution to the impossible bind of low wages and a lack of social services. As inequality has skyrocketed and as public budgets have been slashed, millions of people have been forced to fill the gap by borrowing. Over the years our society has moved from a welfare state to "debtfare" state, with what should be publicly financed goods (universal healthcare, higher education) treated as individual debt obligations. We have to borrow for basic necessities including housing, transportation, schooling, and medical treatment. Even incarceration has become a form of financial extraction, as time in jail and prison now means escalating fines and fees for everything from court appearances and probation costs to "room and board."

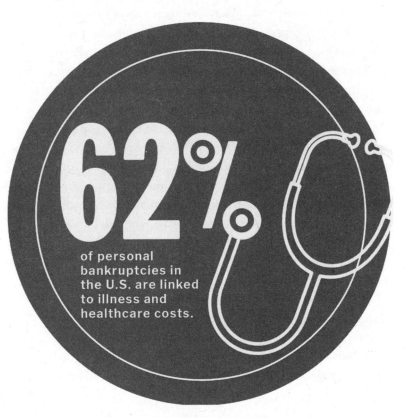

62%
of personal
bankruptcies in
the U.S. are linked
to illness and
healthcare costs.

As a result, more than three quarters of Americans are now in hock. Between 1980 and 2007, household debt doubled as a percentage of GDP, with most of the growth in residential mortgages, although auto, credit card, student loan, medical, and criminal legal debt also grew precipitously. In the first months of 2020, as the pandemic took hold, household debt rose to $14.3 trillion, $1.6 trillion higher than the record set in the middle of the financial crisis. Today, more than 40 percent of indebted households use credit cards to cover basic living costs, including rent, food, and utilities. Some 62 percent of personal bankruptcies in the US are linked to illness and health care costs.

In 2019, US students graduated from college with an average of $32,000 in debt. Those without access to a bank account are harshly penalized. Ten percent of families spend money on alternative financial services such as check cashers (outlets that cash checks, for a fee) and payday lenders (lenders whose high interest loans trap desperate borrowers in endless cycles of debt). You might think that schoolchildren would escape the horror of debt, but you would be wrong. A 2019 report showed that the median amount of debt incurred by children whose families cannot afford their school lunches has increased 70 percent in the last few years.

DEBTORS' REVOLTS

In the coming pages we will go behind the numbers to dig into the economic system that has produced debt for the majority and unimaginable riches for a tiny few. But this book isn't just about the problem of debt. It is also about how to fight back.

Mass indebtedness presents an opening for a new form of resistance to capitalist exploitation. To put it in words often attributed to J. Paul Getty: "If you owe the bank $100,000, the bank owns you. If you owe the bank $100 million, you own the bank." If you add up all of our debt, we own the bank.

Throughout history indebtedness has been a catalyst for rebellion. Debt and debtors' revolts have a long history that predates capitalism. In ancient Greece, during the sixth century BCE, an uprising of the poor compelled the famed aristocrat Solon to end debt slavery in order to avert a social crisis. A century later, in Rome, a surge of indebtedness helped spur the Secession of the Plebs, the mass strikes by commoners that led to the creation of *tribuni plebis*, or tribunes of the people.

In a later age, various American colonies were a magnet for the insolvent. Shays' Rebellion and other debtor revolts struck fear into the hearts of many of the American founding fathers, inspiring James Madison to rail against the "wicked project" of debt abolition in the *Federalist Papers* and leading some scholars to refer to the US Constitution as a "creditors' constitution." The founding fathers knew quite a bit about the power of credit and debt, which they wielded as a weapon to dispossess indigenous people and as a means to profit further from slavery. The question has always been who would get to wield debt as a form of power—the wealthy or the working class?

Occupy Wall Street continued this long-standing pattern. In 2012, soon after the Occupy Student Debt Campaign held a protest marking "1T Day," the day when student loan debt hit the $1 trillion mark, New York City activists took inspiration from a student strike in Québec and organized the first local debtors' assembly. There was a palpable spark as people testified for more than two hours, many noting that they had never before spoken publicly about their financial burden. They recounted ambulance bills that sunk their finances, job losses that caused them to depend on credit, and loans taken out to help loved ones. A deeply personal issue was being politicized before everyone's eyes. The epiphany that suddenly connects an individual experience to a collective condition speaks to one of the Debt Collective's slogans: "You are not a loan."

Similar assemblies held across the country laid the groundwork for the Debt Collective. One of the goals of those assemblies was to transform the dominant understanding of indebtedness in America. This was no easy task. Before the Occupy movement arrived on the scene, debt was a topic more often taken up by the political right, who used the national debt as an excuse to cut social services, even as they increased the deficit through massive tax cuts and bloated military budgets.

Ten years later, the evidence is in: when debtors organize together, we can win, and those achievements can set the stage for even bigger victories. As a consequence of the Corinthian debt strike as well as a complementary legal campaign focused on a little known right called defense to repayment, Debt Collective members have won more than one billion dollars in student loan cancellation for tens of thousands of people. They have also forced some Democrats to embrace student debt cancellation and free public college. When presidential hopeful Elizabeth Warren released a proposal to cancel a portion of federal student loans in 2019, one of her former policy advisors credited the Debt Collective. In her words, our organizing had demonstrated that "sometimes debt just has to be wiped away."

A few months later presidential candidate Bernie Sanders, along with congresswomen Pramila Jayapal, Ilhan Omar, and Alexandria Ocasio-Cortez, invited Debt Collective strikers to speak at an event in Washington, DC, to announce their College for All Act. The bill proposed to cancel all student debt and make public higher education free. On June 24, 2019, it was none other than Pam Hunt who stood at a lectern steps away from the United States Capitol Building, speaking forcefully into the microphone: "I stand before you as a person who pursued a higher degree and was made worse off because of it," she said. "I am not asking for forgiveness, I am demanding justice." Six months later Pam's for-profit college loans were finally abolished. Freed from this obligation, she said she felt that she had gotten her future back.

In addition to wiping out unjust loans, the Debt Collective's student debt strike helped change federal regulations, making it possible, for the first time, for defrauded student borrowers to get their debt discharged. That victory is particularly significant because student loans are the only kind of debt that individuals cannot discharge in bankruptcy, thanks to reforms passed in 1998 and 2005 at the behest of lenders and their lobbyists. None other than Joe Biden led the charge for the 2005 change—not surprising for a former senator from Delaware, the credit card capital of the country.

In the wake of the Coronavirus outbreak, organized campaigns by groups of debtors are more necessary than ever before. At the time of this writing, a version of a mass debt strike is already underway. Millions of individuals and households have stopped paying their debts because they can no longer afford to do so. For the most part, though, this mass nonpayment event was not coordinated and people were isolated from others in their situation. The challenge is turning scattered, spontaneous strikes and uprisings into a coherent, collective, strategic force so debtors can, at long last, assert their will.

We need a politicized bloc of debtors that can go beyond discrete actions and build enduring, collective power. Debtors unions can and should make a range of immediate demands: from caps on interest rates to write-downs or full cancellation of all manner of debts, including credit cards, student loans, and mortgages; from eliminating racist lending practices to a ban on money bail and extractive criminal punishment fees. Mass debt cancellation—what has long been called a "jubilee"—would be a significant victory, but only if coupled with a deep, durable shift in the distribution of political and economic power. If debtors are strategic enough, we can help rewrite the social contract so it centers what we call "reparative public goods"—public goods that ensure our collective well-being by centering the repair and redress of intergenerational theft of land and livelihood from Native, Black, and brown communities. By prioritizing redress and repair, we can win free and universal education, housing, and healthcare. No one should have to go into debt to meet their basic needs.

There has never been a better time for people who hold debt of all kinds to come together, refuse to pay, and demand an economy that works for the vast majority instead of the few. Transforming our world's economic system is a big ambition, but that's what we need to do, for one another and for our planet. As things stand, a few make enormous fortunes from exploitation while our government enables debt vultures to profit from our pain. (In the case of student debt and criminal punishment system debt, the government is itself the debt vulture.) Under today's conditions, declining to pay back debts is a defensible act of civil disobedience. We call it economic disobedience. For those aiming to make a more just society, cultivating such acts of collective refusal may amount to a moral responsibility and a strategic imperative.

CHAPTER ONE

YOU ARE NOT A LOAN: RECOGNIZING OUR POWER IN THE AGE OF DEBT

M ost people are not in debt because they live beyond their means; they are in debt because they have been denied the means to live.

The fact that employers refuse to provide living wages enables creditors to loan more money, with interest, to desperate workers. In this sense, our bosses and lenders collude to rob us twice: first, by underpaying us, and then by charging us interest to borrow the money we need to make ends meet.

Look at this graph illustrating the relationship between productivity and wages.

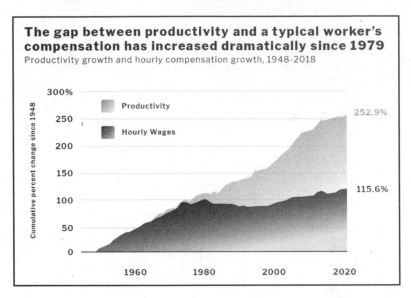

The gap between productivity and a typical worker's compensation has increased dramatically since 1979

Productivity growth and hourly compensation growth, 1948-2018

Since World War II the wealth we produce has been going up and up and up, but our wages have remained stagnant since the mid-1970s. Although we are working longer hours, a growing number of us are forced to cobble together multiple jobs and side hustles. While our work is producing more wealth than ever before, that wealth is being captured by the 1 percent. The pie has been getting bigger, but our slice has stayed the same or shrunk. A full eight out of every ten dollars we produce goes into the pockets of the richest 1 percent.

The Coronavirus pandemic revealed just how out of touch elites are when it comes to most people's household budgets. In the spring of 2020, after millions had lost their jobs and food banks were feeding record numbers of people, Speaker of the

House Nancy Pelosi appeared on a late night comedy show to joke about how much gourmet ice cream she had stored in one of her two freezers. That same week, treasury secretary Steven Mnuchin appeared on cable news to tout the Trump administration's "stimulus" package, consisting largely of one-time $1,200 payments to individuals. In a "let them eat cake" moment for the ages, Mnuchin said he believed the package would "provide economic relief for about ten weeks." He failed to mention that the US Treasury made it legal for banks to seize those meager checks for outstanding debts.

Our lives cannot be improved by following the glib prescriptions that have long come from on high. Consider the sample budget created by financial advisors at the Visa credit card company for McDonald's employees, which claimed to show how it was possible to live on a fast-food worker's income.

The first thing to notice is that they immediately concede that living on a McDonald's salary can't be done. The budget

Sample Monthly Budget	
Monthly Net Income	
Income (1st job)	$ 1,105
Income (2nd job)	$ 955
Other Income	$ 0
Monthly Net Income Total	$ 2,060
Monthly Expenses	
Savings	$ 100
Mortgage/Rent	$ 600
Car Payment	$ 150
Car/Home Insurance	$ 100
Health Insurance	$ 20
Heating	$ 0
Cable/Phone	$ 100
Electric	$ 90
Other	$ 100
Monthly Expenses Total	$ 1,260
Monthly Spending Money	$ 800
(Monthly Net Income Total minus Monthly Expenses Total)	
Daily Spending Money Goal	$ 27
(Monthly Spending Money divided by 30)*	

*the average of 30 days in a month is used to simplify your budget

English | 4

requires a second job that pays almost as much as the primary one. *No worries,* they seem to be saying, *you'll sleep when you're dead!* Some of the budget lines are impossible flights of fancy, like monthly rent of $600 a month, something less likely in many major cities than finding a unicorn. Even more absurd, the budget allows $0 for heat and it doesn't mention food. It seems being responsible means freezing and not eating.

Visa's guidelines demonstrate why the advice of experts who preach financial "literacy" and "responsibility" is so insidious. To personal finance gurus, whose existence is dependent on *not* criticizing the rules of the game, being a good person means working multiple jobs, taking on debt to fill the gaps, and never questioning the arrangement. They want you to work and to be as obedient and profitable to bosses and creditors as possible.

THE MYTH OF THE "GOOD" DEBTOR

Our economy is built on lies. We are told that debt offers an opportunity to get ahead when, in reality, most people spend their entire lives stuck on the debt treadmill. *Take out student loans to go to college so you can graduate and get a good job; borrow money so you can build your credit score and buy more stuff; take out a mortgage so you can become a homeowner; become an entrepreneur with a small business loan.* Debt is presented as a crucial rung on the ladder to a better life, a stepping stone to the American dream. If we can't dig our way out of these "good" debts, we are to blame. But the fact is that most people can't dig themselves out—three-quarters of people take their debts to the grave. On average, Americans die holding $62,000 of debt.

The capitalist fable of upward mobility has always been an illusion. While leveraging debt has lifted some out of poverty (access to credit was a cornerstone of policies that helped create the white middle class), the majority has been left behind or pushed into predatory contracts they can never escape. Debt, however, is more than a trap. It's a form of social control. To give just one example, in 2019 the US Army actually admitted that they exceed their recruiting goals by targeting students in debt. As army recruiting Command Major General Frank Muth put it, "One of the national crises right now is student loans, so $31,000 is [about] the average. [. . .] You can get out [of the Army] after four years, 100 percent paid for state college anywhere in the United States." To be indebted makes us vulnerable to predators of all kinds, including predatory lenders, predatory debt collectors, and predatory military recruiters.

In myriad ways, debt erodes our freedom and forces unbearable choices on us: should I pay my mortgage or pay for my chemotherapy? Should I take out loans to pay for college or enlist in the army to get financial aid? Should I put the groceries on a credit card or be late with rent? Should I go to a payday lender or sleep in my car? We internalize the narrative that we have taken on debt freely and the burden is ours alone to bear when nothing could be further from the truth.

To be indebted is typically a shameful experience. We are hounded by collectors via telephone and mail, our credit scores plummet, and, along with them, our chances for housing, loans, and even employment. Our self-esteem, self-worth, and physical and mental health take a dive too. Being indebted weighs on the body and the mind, stressing us out and making us ill. That's not an accident.

A loan is a weapon for making us feel powerless. Mortgages are a good example. In 1914 Ford Motor Company embarked on a new experiment that gave it nearly dictatorial power over its workers. Henry Ford created his own secret police force and gave it the Orwellian name "Ford Sociological Department." The job of this department was to spy intrusively on factory workers and their families to make sure they were sufficiently conforming to Ford's ideas about the American way of life. This meant an emphasis on thrift and upright moral living (no gambling and certainly no political agitating). Among other things, they wanted to know how much money each worker had saved, in which banks, how much debt they owed, and to whom.

The investigators especially discouraged renting out rooms, even to recent immigrants who were also working at Ford, and pressured employees to buy their own homes and helped them find a mortgage. Why would they care about this? What difference did it matter to management if their employees rented or owned a home? First, they discouraged taking on boarders because, despite the gospel of thrift, they didn't want the workers to have additional sources of revenue. They wanted workers to be completely dependent on the income from their factory job. They also discouraged workers' wives from working for money, both to serve the ideal of a lone male breadwinner and to make the entire household dependent on a single factory income. Second, forcing people into mortgages made them docile workers, unlikely to join a labor strike or cause trouble because doing so might jeopardize their ability to pay their mortgage. Anyone who didn't conform to the Ford Sociological Department's strict standards could have their pay docked and be placed on probation until they "turned their lives around," or they could be fired outright if they resisted this control over their daily lives. Mortgage debt meant that Ford could take away more than just workers' jobs—he could threaten their shelter, too.

Today our privatized healthcare system serves a similar function, even if it is less explicit. Linking medical coverage to employment keeps workers docile and forces unions to spend more of their resources fighting for adequate and affordable health care instead of higher pay, shorter shifts, and real worker ownership of businesses. Many people are tethered to jobs they despise and can't leave because they need the privatized insurance accessed through their employer. After all, one thing worse than a job you hate may be not having one, especially if you have a pre-existing condition that puts your life at risk. Everyone knows that if you are not insured, a single accident can lead to a mountain of hospital bills. More than a third of Americans have medical debt.

When COVID-19 hit, people weren't just afraid of contracting a deadly illness—they were also afraid of losing their jobs along with their insurance, and tens of millions did overnight. In the months before the outbreak, centrist Democrats and their allies worked hard to attack universal health care.

For example, in early February 2020, the leadership of the Culinary Union, which represents casino workers, came out against Medicare for All, arguing that it would cause their membership to lose their private insurance. (In the end membership bucked their leaders and voted overwhelmingly for senator Bernie Sanders, who supported Medicare for All.) One month later the casinos were shut down by the crisis. Even though these casinos got a hefty bailout, more than sixty thousand culinary workers were out of a job and without health care coverage. The pandemic put the pathologies of the American employer-driven, for-profit, debt-producing system of private insurance on display for all to see. In response to the global crisis, industry analysts predicted that health care premiums were set to rise by 40 percent, ensuring ever more people will pay for medical treatment with credit cards.

Debt, in this sense, is a kind of cover-up. Our private contracts, and our desperate attempts to be "good" debtors, all work to conceal a larger crime: the crime of treating health care, shelter, and education as profit centers. Think about the idealistic young student who wants to become a lawyer so they can fight for justice and protect those who have been harmed. By the time they get out of law school, they are looking at six figures of student debt. They could become a public defender—or they could enter corporate law. A corporate law salary allows them a path to pay off their loans. Suddenly the whole reason they wanted to study law in the first place has been replaced with its polar opposite. Eighty percent of Harvard Law School students, to use just one example, enter law school saying they want to practice public interest law. Yet, upon graduation, 80 percent of them go on to practice corporate law. ("But there's a Public Service Loan Forgiveness program to address just this problem!" you might say. To date, the government has denied more than 99 percent of those who have applied to get their loans discharged through this program.)

This isn't just the brainwashing of the Ivy League—although there certainly is a fair amount of that, too—this is the disciplinary function of debt. Most of us want to be better people than we are allowed to be. We are forced to do things we are ethically opposed to, just to survive. We have to service our loans instead of serving the greater good.

FROM DIVESTMENT TO DEBT

The myth of the debtor as an individual who made a bad choice obscures the reason that we are in debt. Medical debt doesn't exist in countries with nationalized health care systems, and student debt is unheard of in parts of the world where public college is free. In the US, the problem is public disinvestment, or what is often called "austerity." Millions who should be eligible for Medicaid, for example, have been pushed off the rolls in recent years. According to one analysis, the number of uninsured children in the US rose by more than four hundred thousand between 2016 and 2018. Disinvestment in the things people need to survive and thrive opens space for profit-hungry predators. In the midst of the

Coronavirus outbreak, the public was shocked to learn that some hospitals were laying off hospital workers and cutting staff salaries while price-gouging patients. Why? Because the hospitals had been acquired by private equity firms, which are in the business of buying companies in order to "restructure" them. For investors, the emergency rooms were not vital public resources but simply cash machines.

Public higher education has also been damaged by "austerity." Public college was free or low cost for much of the twentieth century, and student debt was too insignificant to measure until the 1990s. Things began to unravel in the 1970s, when more people, particularly Black and brown people, demanded access to educational opportunities. In response, states started reducing subsidies to public colleges, and elected officials began talking about public education as a private benefit. A main architect of this shift was California governor Ronald Reagan, who declared war on students at the University of California, whom he called "beatniks, radicals, and filthy speech advocates." He sent in the National Guard to put a stop to student protests and insisted that raising tuition was necessary to quell dissent. Since then, state revenue at public institutions has cratered. Subsidies to schools like Michigan State, the University of Illinois, and the University of California at Berkeley were reduced by more than half between 1987 and 2012. The University of California as a whole now receives only 9 percent of its budget from the state, a massive, decades-long disinvestment campaign that has caused tuition to skyrocket.

Decades of disinvestment in public education has opened up space for predatory for-profit colleges, which are notorious for preying on low-income students, people of color, first-generation students, veterans, and single mothers. Promising a better future, these companies do little more than load students up with loans in order to line the pockets of executives and shareholders.

In area after area, what should be public goods are financed by private debt, with disastrous consequences. Invisible webs of debt wrap around every asset and siphon value from every exchange, allowing the richest among us to profit from the relative poverty of others. Never forget: *your debt is someone else's asset.* Bits of our student loan, mortgage, credit card, and auto loan payments are pooled in order to make money for investors around the world. Bundled with the debt of others, your promise to repay is bought and sold, sliced and diced and speculated on.

And yet we are still sold the lie that debt is a moral relationship between a single creditor and a single debtor. In reality, when a bill collector calls and harasses you, they are probably working for a company that bought your debt for pennies on the dollar from a debt broker. Vultures preying on you to make a buck, they are often willing to break the law to do so. The vast majority of collectors lack the basic paperwork they need to collect legally, yet they issue threats, take people to court, and sometimes land debtors in jail.

Debtors are not just in the red, we're in the dark. This is one important problem that debtors' unions can address.

Many debtors don't know who profits when they pay their debts, or who stands to lose if they don't. Creditors don't want us to understand our debts, which is why we're always told that finance is too complex for regular people to understand. The powerful don't want their schemes to be exposed.

We're in the dark in another sense. Debtors don't know one another. We are isolated and kept apart. Unlike workers organized in a labor union, where a workplace provides a common meeting place, debtors are dispersed far and wide. This is another challenge debtors' unions must overcome—helping people who are being taken advantage of by common creditors to find each other, so we can fight back together instead of being picked off one by one.

Historically, *credit* means *trust*—the act of letting someone borrow resources with the good faith they'll pay you back later when their circumstances have improved. But today, credit is not about trust; it's about extraction. It is hard to overstate just how fundamental trust is to being human. Even the financial terminology hints at this. A financial "trust" is, underneath it all, about real trust. Debtor organizing and debt strikes, just like labor strikes, require building a different kind of trust in one another.

To be clear, relationships of credit and debt are not essentially evil. In fact, debt and credit can and should expand the possibilities of the present, allowing households and communities to access the goods and services they need to thrive. Imagine a city or state borrowing from public banks, not Wall Street, to build infrastructure, such as high-speed trains or schools, so residents can live better in the long term. Too often, though, debt limits our prospects, binding us in chains of compound interest. We mortgage our individual lives for the chance of making it through the day instead of enriching our collective future.

THE TIE THAT BINDS

Disinvestment in public health and welfare has deadly consequences. When people don't earn enough money to care for their families, when they lack access to quality health care, education and other resources, they seek relief any way they can. Drug and alcohol addiction have seen a precipitous rise in recent years, resulting in an increase in what authors Ann Case and Angus Deaton called "deaths of despair." In 2017 alone the number of such deaths totaled 158,000. "The equivalent," the authors wrote, "of three full 737 MAXs falling out of the sky *every day,* with no survivors." Suicide rates have also exploded, increasing every year for the last thirteen years. Unsurprisingly, the Centers for Disease Control and Prevention warned that working-class people were at highest risk of premature death. In 2016, a landmark study showed that the richest American men now live an average of fifteen years longer than the poorest 1 percent of the population.

Though some are better off than others, economic insecurity and its attendant physical and psychic costs are cross-class phenomena. The fear of being laid off or of being unable to access health care when you need it impacts people higher up the income ladder, too, sparing only the truly affluent. Even those who have a financial cushion—a decent salary and maybe some savings or family support to fall back on—are increasingly aware that their own livelihoods are precarious and may be snatched away in an instant, as we saw when the Coronavirus pandemic swept the country.

Many professionals who could formerly count on a decent, secure standard of living have seen their fields decimated. College degree holders are supposed to be insulated from economic downturns. But in recent years, they have felt the squeeze. According to the Economic Policy Institute, some graduates now earn lower wages than they did ten years ago. Anyone who tells you that a college degree is protection from financial ruin is living a fantasy. Those who work in higher education have taken a big hit. Since 2011, 94 percent of all college professors have been hired off the tenure track, meaning that millions of college students are now being taught by faculty who are paid as freelancers and whose only real connection to their school may be an email address. Journalism has been another casualty of decades of privatization. More than five hundred daily newspapers have gone out of business in the last forty years. Other media outlets have been stripped for parts and sold off to corporations. Lawyers are also feeling the pinch. The American Bar Association published statistics showing that lawyers graduate with an average of $110,000 in student loans while salaries after graduation average about $53,000. With no way to repay the loans that supposedly provide an on-ramp to well-paying jobs, many professional careers are closed to all but the most privileged.

It is increasingly clear that capitalism needs us to be insecure and scrambling. This is why labor unions have been under attack for decades and why union membership is on the decline. Employers need employees, and they also need them to live in terror of losing their jobs because fear prevents people from demanding more. This bludgeoning of US workers led Alan Nasser, a professor of political economy, to note that "economic recovery is now treated as consistent with declining standards of living." In other words, when Wall Street touts a recovery, what they are really saying is that they have forced the rest of us to live with even less than we had before. Except debt. That we can have more of.

Soon after the Coronavirus shut down the economy, debt collectors brazenly used the language of diversity to describe themselves as "essential" to the US economy. One lobbying group for the industry fought back against efforts to stop debt collection during the crisis, arguing that halting collections would negatively "impact the diverse workforce that makes up the collection industry," specifically the women and people of color they employ at poverty wages. Their argument was especially insidious since it is precisely women and people of color who are disproportionately impacted by consumer debt, or what we prefer to call household debt, since it typically impacts everyone in a household. During the pandemic, the collection industry wrapped its institutional power in the language of inclusion as a weapon to maintain its profits.

We need to aim for much more than inclusion in a predatory system. Debtors have much in common to build upon so we can push for structural transformation. Debt is the tie that binds the 99 percent, but we also must recognize that it binds some more harshly than others. Debt is not an equalizer; rather it is an intensifier of pre-existing inequalities. Those who are most likely to be indebted are people who have less intergenerational family wealth, whose lands and livelihoods have been stolen due to discrimination, and whose inclusion in the financial system is often predatory. That means poor people, Black and brown people, trans people, and immigrant communities suffer disproportionately under the current system.

The fact that we are all in hock to creditors does not change the different ways that racism, patriarchy, and ableism continue to affect our everyday lives. It does, however, open up the possibility of new, powerful alliances. Mass indebtedness is a social condition that lays the groundwork for the kind of cross-class, multiracial coalition we desperately need to actually target capitalism, not just its symptoms. We can respond to our circumstances with fear and competition or with indignation and cooperation, transforming our accumulated debt into accumulated power to forge a new path.

FORECLOSURE KINGS

Some people might worry that campaigns of economic disobedience and debt refusal encourage irresponsible behavior. *Are you telling me that I can buy whatever I want on a credit card and then just refuse to pay it?* It is true that some individuals are irresponsible with their personal finances, but they tend not to be your average debtors. Congressman Newt Gingrich famously carried a balance of half a million dollars on his line of credit at Tiffany's because he liked to buy expensive jewelry he couldn't afford. That's an example of someone who doesn't know how to balance a budget. Senator Marco Rubio got himself into financial trouble when, already deep in debt, he spent eighty thousand dollars on a luxury boat because he couldn't resist fulfilling a childhood dream. Before she became secretary of education, Betsy DeVos funded a front group called "All Children Matter" aimed at privatizing education. This group violated all kinds of laws and was slapped with a $6 million fine by the courts. Instead of paying that debt, DeVos simply dissolved "All Children Matter" and walked away from her obligations. Betsy DeVos doesn't have to pay her debts, but poor people do.

It's time to challenge the phony morality around debt. At the very top of the wealth pyramid, the rules that keep the little people in line don't apply. Companies and the individuals they have made rich walk away from their debts all the time, thanks to bankruptcy laws and government bailouts. More than anyone else, Donald Trump exemplifies this double standard. He famously declared bankruptcy six times. It takes a special kind of loser to lose money running a casino where the house always wins, and yet Donald Trump managed to do it.

These egregious double standards were on full display during the 2008 mortgage crisis, when a large percentage of homes in the US were underwater, meaning that the real value of the house was lower than the mortgage. Homeowners, predictably, did not lose out equally. African-American families lost 53 percent of their collective wealth and Latinx communities 66 percent percent, far more than their white counterparts. Nonwhite people have long been preyed upon by unscrupulous lenders, and the housing bubble of the 2000s was no exception. Quantitative data analysis shows that the mortgage crash represented one of the largest destructions of the wealth of people of color in US history.

The same can't be said for the financiers. JP Morgan Chase took $12 billion in bailout cash, which transformed public money into private wealth and massive bonuses. When the rich make bad business decisions and their gambles don't pay off, they shirk their financial obligations while the rest of us pay for it. It's just good business. But what about homeowners who were in an underwater mortgage? Why couldn't they just walk away from their debt like a high-rolling CEO? JP Morgan's CEO Jamie Dimon scoffed at the prospect. In a live television interview, he said that an underwater mortgage holder had to stay put: "They're supposed to pay the mortgage, and we should teach the American people, you're supposed to meet your obligations, not run from them. Because you have a mortgage doesn't mean you should run away as it goes down." In other words, even though Dimon's company got bailed out and evaded its own debt, the rest of us can't do the same.

Meanwhile, in Iceland, where the situation was even worse, they took a radically different approach. Instead of bailing out the banks, Iceland put the bankers in jail. They also implemented a jubilee—a form of mass debt cancellation—and required "principal corrections" to bring down the price of mortgages so they were closer to the real value of the homes. The result was a speedy economic turnaround. In the United States, in contrast, it was mainly Wall Street that rebounded successfully. Today, the financial sector is bigger and more influential than it was before the crash, thanks to policies pursued by the Obama administration. Obama's lead financial advisors included Larry Summers and Robert Rubin, who had both been instrumental in the 1999 repeal of the Glass-Steagall Act, a Great Depression–era reform implemented by President Roosevelt to create a firewall between retail and investment banking in order to protect regular depositors.

Summers's and Rubin's decisions set the stage for the massive bailout package to come. After the housing market crash, corporations began buying back their corporate stock, resulting in windfall profits to executives and shareholders. Corporations spent nearly $2.5 trillion on these buybacks in the years 2018 and 2019 alone, much of it financed by debt. Companies borrowed like crazy, capitalizing on the Fed's bargain-basement interest rates. In 2019 corporate debt topped $16 trillion.

Buying back all that stock meant that companies were not well prepared when the COVID-19 pandemic hit. Congress once again stepped in to save the day, quickly passing the CARES Act and flooding corporations with public money. (Journalist David Dayen called the program a trillion-dollar "bazooka aimed at CEOs and shareholders, with almost no conditions attached.") As tens of millions of working people applied for unemployment and/or lined up at food banks, and the pot of money that was supposed to go to small businesses ran out, corporations were swiftly rescued from their poor financial decisions and rewarded for their selfish, short-term thinking. In a move similar to 2008, when credit-rating agencies gave the AAA seal of approval to the toxic mortgage assets that tanked the economy, risky corporate bonds got high ratings, despite the fact that these companies were so laden with debt they couldn't survive a downturn without an influx of federal aid.

When questioned about the Federal Reserve's decision to purchase the junk bonds—that is, the debt—of companies whose investment ratings had toppled due to the pandemic, Fed chair Jerome Powell referred to newly distressed companies as "fallen angels." This leniency is at odds with the role that corporate debt played in creating the current crisis. Over-leveraged companies made our economy more vulnerable to the Coronavirus shock. Yet instead of being sanctioned, their greedy behavior is being rewarded with government handouts.

The rest of us are held to a different standard. Being even a few days late on a monthly payment will ding our credit scores and might even cause us to lose our homes. A little over a decade ago that's what happened to a ninety-year-old woman who owed thirty cents to California's OneWest bank—a bank whose then CEO was none other than Steven Mnuchin, the man who would later be appointed treasury secretary by

Donald Trump. OneWest was engaged in extensive illegal behavior including, according to one report, "backdating documents, rigging foreclosure auctions, and gaming statutes." (Mnuchin also allegedly sent one homeowner's name to a debt collector who proceeded to call her eighty-one times in a single day.) When the Federal Deposit Insurance Corporation (FDIC) backed bank losses during the crisis, OneWest used the windfall to pad the pockets of executives. Flash forward to 2020, as a result of the Coronavirus crisis, the man who earned the title the "Foreclosure King" got promoted to Bailout Emperor, presiding over a multitrillion-dollar corporate slush fund with near total discretion as to who would receive the money and under what terms.

Trump's son-in-law, Jared Kushner, wasted no time seizing the opportunity to cash in. Tasked with helping to oversee the White House's Coronavirus response, Kushner also demanded rent from his tenants and asked for leniency from his creditors. Kushner's real estate business sent debt collectors to extract payments during the pandemic and continued to file eviction lawsuits despite the fact that the governors of New Jersey and Maryland, where Kushner owned real estate, had called for eviction moratoriums.

Like Obama and his Wall Street allies in 2008, Trump and his corporate cronies turned an economic calamity into a rich-get-richer opportunity. But the reality is the corporate executives don't need a crisis to exploit debt to their advantage. Everyday capitalism gives them plenty of opportunities to make a buck by screwing over everyone else. Private equity firms are a prime example. They engage in leveraged buyouts (where borrowed money is used to acquire a company) and then impose the "discipline of debt" to force managers to focus more relentlessly on generating shareholder rewards while the company is sold for parts. Workers pay the ultimate cost while investors cash out and, even here, only some investors are made whole. Pensioners are rarely first in line when private equity firms drive corporations out of business. And guess which "essential" industry demanded and received bailout money in 2020? You guessed it: private equity.

While regular people waited for paltry $1,200 checks, Wall Street speculators and billionaires like Virgin Airlines founder Richard Branson lined up at the government trough demanding a handout. The opulently wealthy are the true "moral hazard" where debt and credit are concerned, since they never bear the full brunt of the risks they take, leaving the rest of us with the tab for their recklessness. Why should ordinary people honor our debts when the rich have walked away from theirs without remorse, or when they have borrowed money for unconscionable aims?

The Debt Collective believes that it is time for debtors to take a page out of the creditors' playbook. The results of the mortgage crisis were so devastating in part because banks and their lobbyists were well organized to fight for debt relief while the rest of us were not. The banks have a powerful collective advocacy operation including lobbyists and a revolving door of regulators and cabinet members who move between the upper echelons of banks and government. The power of mortgage lenders became more apparent during the Obama administration, when the president announced the creation of the Home Affordable Modification Program (HAMP), which was supposed to help three to four million distressed homeowners. This was a government-initiated program that ended up farming out the job of mortgage relief to the same predatory industry that caused the crisis in the first place, resulting in the denial of assistance to 70 percent of the 5.7 million people who applied.

In 2008, Sheila Bair, the Republican head of the FDIC during the crisis, bucked the bipartisan wisdom of the day and argued that homeowners should be bailed out. Imagine if she had had the backing of a nationwide union of mortgage holders. If debtors had been organized, they might have been able to demand relief while assuring that the bankers paid for the crisis they created. They might have been able to demand positive changes, including the end of predatory and racist lending practices, more and better public housing, and stricter rules protecting renters from eviction during an economic downturn. These are the kinds of fights that might have helped millions prepare for the next crisis. If there is one thing that the last twelve years have taught us, it is that debtors must get organized, not only to protect people in the here and now but also to help us all get ready for the battles to come.

JUST AND UNJUST DEBTS

The United States has more wealth than any country in the history of the world. Yet US residents are subjected to wages that force us into poverty, long hours at jobs that steal more and more of our time, an economic system that is poisoning our planet and threatening our extinction, endless wars, and the imprisonment of one out of every thirty-seven adults, disproportionately Black and brown men.

These are serious, existential crises. The good news is that we have the resources to address these problems, to abolish the prisons, liberate ourselves from meaningless and harmful work, fund our healthcare and schools, redistribute our land, and decarbonize our economy. The problem is that we need to redirect public wealth to the reparative common good. We must stop paying illegitimate debts imposed on us from above and honor the real debts we owe. One of the first steps is to realize and acknowledge that our debts to creditors are illegitimate. The second step is to identify our *legitimate* debts to one another.

Distinguishing between *just* and *unjust* debts is a kind of moral audit. Martin Luther King Jr., and many before and since, made a distinction between just and unjust laws. We have a moral obligation to obey just laws or to cooperate with the people who impose them. But we also have an equal moral obligation to disobey unjust laws and to refuse to cooperate with the system that produces them. We should make the same distinction between just and unjust debts. An unjust debt is one that people are forced into in order to meet a basic need. We all need healthy food, clean water to drink, clean air, and a stable ecosystem. We all need a safe place to live. We will all get injured and sick and need health care, and we all need access to education to fully develop our minds and characters and to think for ourselves. No one should be forced into debt because they want to get an education or because they went to jail or because they got cancer or because they can't afford food or shelter.

In contrast, a *just* debt is one that increases the power, increases the wealth, and increases the freedom of those entering into it. For example, we owe profound debts to indigenous peoples and African descendants across the world whose lands and labor funded the global expansion of capitalism, an economic system "dripping from head to toe, from every pore, with blood and dirt," as Marx once wrote. The entire US economy, and indeed the entire global economy, is built on stolen land and unpaid slave labor. These are debts that emanate from our world's deepest injustices, and they must be paid. Reparations are long overdue.

We use the phrase "debt abolition" intentionally. It was Dylan Rodríguez—professor and cofounder of Critical Resistance, a prison abolition organization—who originally posed this question to us: What would it mean to take the abolition in "debt abolition" seriously? First, we have to think about what abolition means today. Guided by the work of Critical Resistance and some of its other cofounders, including Ruth Wilson Gilmore and Angela Davis, we understand abolition as a strategy and a vision for a world without police, prisons, border control, and the current carceral system. But abolition is not only about dismantling oppressive structures, or for a world *without*. Abolition is a strategy and a vision for a world *with* social housing, health care, education, art, and meaningful work, and a life free from state violence and material want. Debt abolition works similarly. It is a vision for a world without exploitative debt contracts, and with socially financed health care, education, housing, and more. Like prison abolition, debt abolition is a strategy and a vision for a world without—and a world with. Indeed, the two forms of abolition may require one another. A world where people can access housing and health care and education and art would have to be a world in which we do not drown in debt for public goods.

When COVID-19 swept the globe, followed by an unprecedented wave of anti–police violence protests, the phrase "debt abolition" began to resonate even more strongly. Both prison abolition and debt abolition challenge the imagination. Lenders canceling debts may seem as unrealistic as prisons releasing prisoners, but both happened in the rise of the pandemic (though not on the scale that we hoped to see). Less than two months into the crisis the United States decarcerated nearly twenty thousand people from jails and prisons. Similarly, household debt contracts that we had long been told were non-negotiable—rent payments, mortgage payments, student debt payments, medical bills, and fines and fees in the criminal punishment system—were suddenly subject to negotiation and delay, as "pauses," "suspensions," and "moratoriums" were granted across the country. When millions rose up in response to the brutal murders of Ahmaud Arbery, Breonna Taylor, and George Floyd at the hands of the state, protesters could be heard demanding that the police be defunded and regular people's debts be canceled.

To borrow inspiration from an unlikely source, economist Milton Friedman, in the opening of *Capitalism and Freedom*, wrote: "Only a crisis—actual or perceived—produces real change. When that crisis occurs, the actions that are taken depend on the ideas that are lying around." This is part of the point of any debtors union: to develop alternatives to existing policies, to keep them alive and available until the politically impossible becomes politically inevitable.

DEBTS HELD IN COMMON

Changing the world requires more than just a radical vision of a different world; it requires solidarity. The word *solidarity* originally meant debt held in common. The idea first emerged in the legal books of the ancient Roman Empire. When people held a debt together, they were said to hold it *in solidum*. In other words, the state of being on the hook as a group was the basis of solidarity. If one individual faltered, the group had to step up—meaning that its members would be either bailing one another out or defaulting together. Thus, from its genesis, solidarity had a financial component that raised the stakes. In this original formulation, solidarity is a common identity and a state of interdependence. Terms like *bonds* and *trust* and *mutual funds* are now used by bankers to describe financial structures and agreements; solidarity can turn such notions around to strengthen the ties among a community of debtors. If just one of us refuses to pay our debt, the state and Wall Street have the power to crush us. But if we all refuse, the power shifts. This kind of organizing cannot be conjured out of thin air; debt strikes cannot be "declared" from on high. But if we see our debt as connecting us to one another and as part of what brings us together in solidarity, then our debt can be a source of power.

Debtors' unions aren't a panacea, but they have an important role to play. Regular people can't afford to leave power on the table—that's why we need to turn our debt into leverage. This is debt's double edge, its dual power. By design it can isolate us and make us feel alone. But if we think of our debt as common, that your medical bill and my credit card debt are both connected by an exploitative system, even by the same bank, then we can refuse these unjust debts in solidarity. We are indebted together, and we can be liberated together. We must build these bonds with one another before we can cut the bonds that tie us to creditors and collectors and to all those who exploit us for profit. We also need to build power. That is why the Debt Collective is not advocating debt "forgiveness"—which implies a benevolent creditor taking pity on a blameworthy debtor—but rather debt *abolition* and the creation of a new economic paradigm in which our individual well-being and shared liberation is a *socially financed* project.

CHAPTER TWO

HOW DID WE GET HERE?
FINANCIALIZATION FROM HAITI TO THE HOUSEHOLD

I f you are reading this book you may have already heard our economic system described as *neoliberal capitalism*. Neoliberalism is a form of capitalism that asserts that human well-being is synonymous with entrepreneurialism, that the "free" market is the best way to organize an economy, and that the state should exist only to protect private property. On a societal scale, this approach produces disastrous consequences: the reckless pursuit of profits, a ransacked and deeply unequal society, and mass indebtedness. But what is the specific mechanism, within neoliberal capitalism, that has resulted in so many of us drowning in debt? To answer that question, we must add a second term to our discussion: *financialization*.

The finance sector of the economy has grown at an astonishing rate over the last few decades to become a dominant and dangerous force in our society. Compensation for financial intermediaries, including banks, hedge funds, and private equity firms, is at an all-time high, approaching 10 percent of GDP. "Profiting without producing," is how some economists describe financialization. In contrast to the regular or "real" economy, which manufactures the goods and provides the services we need to live—and where many of the "essential workers" who were required to stay on the job during the pandemic are employed—the financial sector is all about finding ways to generate revenue without creating anything tangible or useful. Over the last four decades, Wall Street has been using fees, interest, and complex financial instruments to skim from the top, taking a larger portion for themselves year after year. Financial returns have become the primary source of wealth accumulation for the rich, who hold paper claims promising them shares of future profits, while everyone else makes due with an ever-shrinking piece of the economic pie. All the money that has been sucked up by executives and shareholders is money that doesn't go to workers, get used to fund actual production, or get invested to secure our present and future well-being, leaving the majority of people poorer and worse off.

Financialization can seem complex when scholars and economists talk about it, but the lived experience is pretty straightforward. For most of us, financialization is experienced as indebtedness. Financialization is when we are forced to borrow to access goods and services, such as medical care and higher education, that the government should guarantee for all. Financialization is when wages are stagnant, but credit cards and other lines of credit are widely available. Financialization is when pension funds get fed into global financial markets and retirees have to pray that the value of their 401Ks stays high. Financialization is when companies obsess over stock prices and offer "buybacks" to their shareholders rather than reinvesting their wealth to expand production and hire more workers. Financialization is when Congress acts to protect creditors, making it harder for people to declare bankruptcy or stop harassment by collectors. Financialization is when communities pay steep fees to borrow money from Wall Street to fund basic infrastructure instead of taxing the affluent. Financialization is when mortgage lenders package loans into bundles called "securities" and then sell them to the highest bidder, crashing the economy. In short, financialization is the name for a set of processes, central to neoliberal capitalism, that have helped to generate huge profits for the creditor class, seemingly out of thin air, by plunging millions of people into debt.

One of the reasons we began organizing around debt is that we believe there's an implicit contradiction in the age of finance: it makes new kinds of collective action possible now that weren't before. The mass indebtedness created by financialization is not only a liability; it is also a collective asset and potential leverage point.

The term *collective* is key. Neoliberalism is built on the myth of the lone entrepreneur, and most financial contracts bind individuals. But few of us live in economic isolation. When we can't pay our bills, we often turn to family for help. Our inability to pay affects our families, and often multiple generations, as we shift resources around to try and make ends meet. Financialization may treat us all as individuals, but once we see that we actually hold these financial contracts together, then we can begin to develop the power to break them, to renegotiate them, to rewrite them, together. Understanding financialization's roots in racism and colonialism is a good place to start.

HUMAN CAPITAL IN HAITI

The economy changed dramatically in the 1970s, when modern financialization began to take hold. That is the period when accounts of financialization typically begin. But finance is nothing new, and putting people into debt has long been indispensable to those in power. The roots of financialization are deep, and tracing them leads us back to the days of colonial conquest and plunder.

The history of a place once called Saint Domingue, now known as Haiti, is instructive. Between 1784 and 1791, the transatlantic slave trade brought a quarter of a million African people to this single Caribbean island, which was then a French colony. *Two hundred and fifty thousand people over merely seven years.* The invention of the power loom a few years earlier, and the faster production it enabled, meant that the British demand for raw cotton was skyrocketing. French and British colonists used enslaved labor in Caribbean cotton fields to feed this demand. But, as has been the case throughout history, people revolted. Between 1791 and 1804, African and Afro-Haitian people in Saint Domingue organized and executed a successful insurrection against French colonial rule, ushering in the sovereign nation of Haiti in 1804.

The revolution changed the course of global capitalism. Along with the abolition of the Atlantic trade in enslaved people that followed in 1808 (though not the abolition of slavery itself, which would come decades later), the Haitian revolution forced European colonial powers and merchants to look elsewhere to meet demand. Britain still needed cotton to feed what the poet William Blake called its "dark satanic mills," and so it turned to the United States.

Plantation owners were eager to satisfy Britain's desire for raw materials, but to do so they needed more land and more labor. The American founding fathers did their part to help. In 1803, Thomas Jefferson told lenders to encourage indigenous people to borrow excessively and then lay claim to their property as collateral. Debt, he argued, could be strategically deployed to force Native Americans to sell their territory. "To promote this disposition to exchange lands," he wrote, "we shall push our trading houses and be glad to see the good and influential individuals among them run in debt." Jefferson, meanwhile, spent most of his life racking up massive personal debts, and upon his death the enslaved people on his estate were sold to pay what he owed.

The idea that human beings have a monetary value, or what some call "human capital," is the essence of financialization.

And it has deep and insidious roots in nineteenth-century transnational finance. Take another example from the same period: How did US planters secure the money they needed to grow all that cotton? British merchants looking to import raw cotton would lend them the capital to buy enslaved people, cottonseed, tools, and food to feed their labor force. After harvest, planters were expected to repay British investors, with interest. (*To finance* something, after all, means to provide capital with the expectation of future profit.) But what if planters had a bad crop that year? Or the price of global cotton fell? Or there was an uprising on their plantation? Meaning, what if the planter couldn't pay back the loan? To make a contemporary analogy, when people can't pay their mortgages, they lose their homes. In finance terminology, the house was *collateral* on the loan, essentially something of value the lender can take if the borrower can't pay. In the nineteenth-century global cotton economy, *people* of African descent were the collateral. If the planter couldn't repay his London-based lender, he owed that lender his enslaved workers. To get a sense of the financial value of this workforce, historian Sven Beckert estimates that the value of enslaved people in the United States in 1860 was equal to *all of the capital invested in American railroads, manufacturing, and agricultural land combined*. In short, the United States emerged as a player in global capitalism through the commodification, theft, and enslavement of indigenous, African, and African-descendent peoples.

Decades of international abolition organizing and anticolonial independence struggles would eventually score significant victories, but at a steep price. Generations of Haitians were forced to pay the price for their predecessors' rebellion. Between 1825 and 1947, the French government imposed an annual payment on Haiti as compensation for slave owners' lost "property." The sum totaled 150 million francs, later reduced to 90 million (an amount estimated to be around $40 billion in today's dollars)· demanded by France for appropriated plantations and military expenditures. (Kenya also began its independence in the 1960s owing a debt of £29 million to the departing British colonists who had stolen the Kenyans' land.) The entire country was punished with permanent debt peonage because the people had fought successfully against enslavement.

In the United States, after abolition, similar tactics were used to target individuals recently liberated from bondage. White landlords imposed unpayable debts via sharecropping and tenant farming arrangements to suppress Black independence while also creating a moral economy in which Black people, instead of being owed reparations for centuries of stolen labor, were turned into debtors who owed white people gratitude for their emancipation.

This is the past we must grasp in order to understand where we are today. Financialization is a contemporary development, but one that relies on wealth that came from the violent, colonialist theft of land, lives, and labor. This ill-gotten wealth has been passed down through generations allowing some to profit from this historical plunder (a phenomenon known as "intergenerational wealth transfer"). Meanwhile,

Black and indigenous people, who start out life in households with fewer assets and resources, on average, than their white counterparts, continue to pay the price.

IT'S ALL HOUSEHOLD DEBT

If the Haitian Revolution is our first unexpected starting point for better understanding financialization, *the household* is our second. The household has long been a basic economic unit (etymologically, the root word of "economy," *oikonomia,* means household management). Today, the intimate relationship between financialization and the family or household routinely compels what can only be described as impossible choices. *Will my liberal arts degree lead to a salary that can cover the debt I and my parents must take on? Do I pay my mortgage or my son's criminal legal fees so that he isn't subject to re-arrest? Do I take out a title loan on my car so my kids have somewhere safe to sleep? Can I afford chemotherapy and avoid foreclosure at the same time?* These devastating calculations are a constant feature of contemporary life, and they always involve more than a single person. In every agonizing choice, the various forms of debt overlap, with cascading consequences for debtors and those they love.

What kind of household we are born into, or choose to create, shapes our experience of both indebtedness and income. Consider the Fordist family wage—the idea dominant in the 1950s and 1960s that a worker on Henry Ford's assembly line should be able to afford the car they produce *and* afford to support their family on that single wage. In her book *Family Values*, sociologist Melinda Cooper shows that the values of Fordism were based around white, male factory workers who were married to women. In other words, in a model that some hold up as the golden era of capitalist production, when more and more workers were joining the middle class, being white and a member of a patriarchal, traditional family qualified people for a living wage and employment protections. As Cooper writes, "the Fordist politics of class . . . established white, married masculinity as a point of access to full social protection." Workers who didn't fit those categories were not entitled to the same wages or social benefits.

Historically, our policy makers have pulled the rug from beneath nontraditional family structures by failing to support other ways to love, care, and create households. This offers another reminder that debt is not an individual failing but a status held by families and communities, with some families and communities more likely to be indebted on predatory terms than others. Debt is *structural*: we are more likely to go into debt if we are members of particularly marginalized groups, including those whose ancestors were enslaved, or whose ancestors' land was stolen by colonizers, and/or who are currently members of nontraditional households and families.

Staying attuned to the structural causes of indebtedness is important because the role of the household has also been transformed in more recent times. Beginning in the mid-1930s, the New Deal established programs like Social Security and Medicare, helping to carve out a path to the American dream of upward mobility, home ownership, and a better life for one's children. The dream would eventually be propped up, in part, by making credit more widely accessible to regular people.

During this period, the federal government invested heavily to build highways and facilities to serve suburban development; it subsidized a mortgage finance program for home ownership, a public university system, and a welfare and health care system for the poor. The society of the 1950s relied on this physical and social infrastructure to subsidize the promise that (some) individuals with a high school education and a good work ethic could achieve middle-class status. As a result of such investment, many services were provided by state and federal governments, and strong labor unions ensured fair wages and benefits. The New Deal era was not perfect, and it left many people out—Black agricultural workers, domestic workers, and single women were often actively excluded from participating in the postwar system of government-funded prosperity, including, most consequentially, the mortgage market. Between 1934 and 1962, 98 percent of the loans insured by the Federal Housing Administration went to white Americans, freezing Black Americans out of the government program that created the white middle class. Nevertheless, the United States entered a short-lived period of economic redistribution as a result of federal government intervention. For the thirty years following World War II, many basic services not provided publicly were affordable on a worker's salary, and it was possible for some, disproportionately white, households to earn incomes sufficient to meet their needs.

This system soon came under attack from multiple angles. Beginning in the 1960s, both the civil rights movement and the women's movement pressed for inclusion in the American dream of opportunity and upward mobility. They demanded access to housing, education, welfare programs, and more access to credit. These expanded demands on resources coincided with the sustained economic crisis of the 1970s, including high inflation, unemployment, and high interest rates. Policy makers were confronted with conflicting but increasingly organized and vocal demands from citizens and workers in a time of slow economic growth. At the same time, employers and business owners began to get organized. Anxious over stagnating profits, they wanted workers to accept less than what the New Deal era had promised them. It was at this messy intersection of social movement demands, political economic crisis, and an increasingly militant working class that a ruling-class backlash began to brew. As part of the turn toward financialization, public policy began to *promote* access to credit as a solution to the problem of ordinary people demanding more of the state.

A number of broad economic policies followed, as the sociologist Greta Krippner shows, including: (1) the deregulation of financial markets, which led banks and creditors to invent new ways to profit from different kinds of loans; (2)

high interest rates at the Federal Reserve under its chairman Paul Volcker, which was the federal government saying it preferred to keep prices low instead of raising wages; (3) policy makers expanding access to consumer credit. Together, these policies helped grow the financial sector of the economy and brought immense profits to creditors, banks, insurance companies, and major corporations. Financialization also meant a shift in corporate practices over the same period. Average CEO pay increased 937 percent between 1978 and 2013 while workers' wages flatlined. Median weekly earnings have grown at only 0.1 percent per year since 1979.

The next year, Ronald Reagan rode a wave of anti-tax sentiment to the White House. Once there he began implementing a neoliberal agenda, and the number of millionaires quickly spiked. In addition to slashing taxes, attacking unions, and deregulating the financial sector, Reagan instituted significant cuts to federal funding for many social safety net programs, including food stamps, school lunch programs, Medicaid, job training, and unemployment benefits. These cuts hurt poor people of color the most and targeted Black women in particular. (Black women had been leading a successful welfare rights movement that was winning benefits and dignity for nontraditional family forms, specifically female-headed households, something rich, sexist, racist men objected to twice over: they didn't like the prospect of increased public spending or Black female empowerment.) As the War on Drugs ramped up in the 1980s, "consumer credit" expanded in increasingly nefarious directions. An explosion in the prison population and incarceration costs led states to charge fees to people accused of a crime. In the following decades, federal, state, and municipal governments began transforming ever more public services into private financial obligations. People were now in debt for everything from going to college to going to jail. This combination of wage stagnation and cuts to social programs produced a new generation of households without the ability to meet the rising cost of living. With the rich refusing to pay their fair share in taxes and public services decimated, regular people had no choice but to rely on a combination of kinship networks and, importantly, credit.

Affluent people are, predictably, far better off under these circumstances, with well-connected relatives and inherited wealth to fall back on. This is another reason the rich have gotten richer. As the economist Thomas Piketty and others have demonstrated, wealth today is not built through accumulated wages but through private inheritance. For example, it is much easier to save money if you inherit a house and do not have to buy one yourself or if you didn't have to take on loans to go to college. If *inheritance* plays such a central role in the distribution of wealth, then we are again looking at the importance of a certain kind of family, and the continuation of rich people passing assets down to their children—intergenerational wealth transfer again—and poor people getting stuck with debt. Of course these disparities are racialized. As journalist Nikole Hannah-Jones has noted, "the average Black family with children holds just one cent of wealth for every dollar that the average white family with children holds."

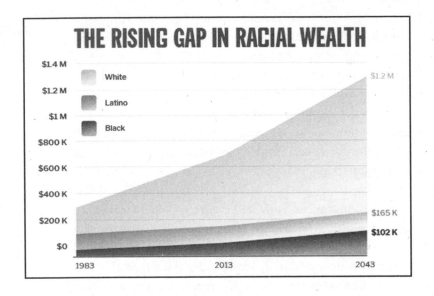

THE RISING GAP IN RACIAL WEALTH

With wealth amassing on one side and debt on the other, the finance sector boomed. Money managers were happy to watch over family fortunes, raking in fees for handling private investments. At the same time, the state's strategy of forcing households to access basic goods through high-cost and high-interest credit was a massive windfall for creditors. The last forty years of financialization have seen the mass distribution of debt, funneling money from working families to Wall Street.

THEY GOT BAILED OUT, WE GOT SOLD OUT

We all suffer from the consequences of financialization. This is the economic system that came to be known as "too big to fail." In reality, it fails us all every day.

In 2008 the pathologies of the system were put on stark display when the global economy collapsed. The crisis was partially triggered by mass defaults on US "subprime" home loans—"nontraditional," predatory mortgages that were more likely to be offered to African American borrowers. A 2012 study found that *even when income and credit risk were equal*, African Americans were up to 34 percent more likely to receive subprime and higher interest loans than their white counterparts. Black women, often single mothers, got hit the worst of all. Women, one study reported, were 32 percent more likely to receive subprime loans than men.

People being preyed upon by unscrupulous lenders is only part of the story. New, shadowy financial markets opened up to profit from the scheme. For more than a decade leading up to the financial crisis, mortgage payments on both prime and subprime loans had been packaged and sold to investors as a product called "mortgaged-backed securities." This secondary market was extremely profitable for investors all over the world, which meant that Wall Street banks had an almost insatiable appetite for *more mortgages*. This demand drove lenders to push people to borrow on predatory terms. This process was driven by investor profits, completely detached from the idea that a home is where we build our lives, care for our loved ones, grieve our losses, and celebrate our joys. Mortgages securitized into global investment products spread the risk that borrowers would default throughout the banking system.

In the years leading up to the 2008 mortgage meltdown, working-class communities of color were a testing ground for unjust financial practices that ultimately became widespread. After decades of being sold predatory mortgages to feed Wall Street greed, millions of people from all backgrounds began struggling to repay their loans. These defaults destabilized the global financial system. Global credit markets froze, and millions lost their homes, jobs, and savings. Between 2006 and 2013, nearly 14 million homes entered the foreclosure process, and more than 9 million American households lost their homes. In an outcome that illustrates how financialization works, more than 28 percent of African American families and 31 percent of Latinx families who bought homes during the subprime boom lost them to foreclosure or were seriously delinquent by January 2013. This was double the rate of non-Hispanic white and Asian households.

This was not the story, though, that was widely told in the media. In a now infamous 2013 cover illustration, *Bloomberg Businessweek* suggested that reckless, financially illiterate borrowers of color caused the housing crisis, and may cause the next one as well. The cover featured racist cartoon caricatures of four people in different rooms of a house, variously appearing to bathe in money, feed money to their dog, or gamble with it like playing cards. The cover story's subtitle read, in part, "What could possibly go wrong?" suggesting plainly that lending to people of color was financially risky because they had borrowed irresponsibly. In other words, long-standing and pervasive stereotypes deflected responsibility for the crisis away from Wall Street and onto individual, pathologized people of color. It was the Reagan-era "Welfare Queen"—a stereotype of Black single-mothers accused of stealing from the state's welfare programs—reemerging in portrayals of the indebted household. Except now she was a debt queen.

INDEBTED FAMILIES, STOLEN FUTURES

Given the history of capitalism and the rise of financialization, the Great Recession that began in 2008 was not an isolated crisis, and the racist mortgage market was not exceptional. Discriminatory disparities hold true across household debt categories, from mortgages to credit cards to auto loans, student loans, and more.

Think about utility bills. What could be more essential to the household than basic utilities like electricity, gas, and water? Water is, of course, a necessity of life. During a pandemic, it becomes even more critical. In early 2020, when COVID-19 began to spread like wildfire around the planet, we were told that washing our hands is the most effective way to keep ourselves and our communities safe. That's sensible advice, if you have access to clean running water.

Unfortunately, millions of US residents don't. In many cases, this is because their water has been shut off due to nonpayment. Water shutoffs for those behind on their bills were recorded in all fifty states in the early weeks of the pandemic, but they were most pronounced in cities like Detroit.

Our household debt often stems from the fact that our cities are indebted (something we'll explore in more detail in the next chapter). In Detroit, the water bill crisis is directly connected to the city's 2013 bankruptcy, which led governor Rick Snyder to appoint an emergency manager named Kevyn Orr. Orr's job was to decide which debts the city of Detroit would pay, and which would not be paid. As the logic of financialization dictated, he decided that the city's pensioners would be forced to take a cut in order to satisfy Wall Street banks and their investors. In order to ensure those financiers got their cut, the city began to aggressively collect property taxes and water bills. Fast forward seven years, and we can see the direct link between the spike in COVID-19 cases and deaths in Detroit and the forced repayment of debts to Wall Street investors. One reason that Detroit had an especially bad outbreak of COVID-19 was that many people could not wash their hands because investors prioritized profits over public health. Your monthly bill is someone else's profit, a reward unrelated to providing an essential service like clean water.

Even if you don't live in Detroit, there's a good chance you have enjoyed the city's water. Both Pepsi (Aquafina) and Coca-Cola (Dasani) have water-bottling operations located there. All they do is take the municipal Detroit water, fill plastic bottles with it, then sell that water at a markup price 113 times what the water costs out of the tap. Both soft-drink companies are often behind on their payments, racking up overdue bills in the hundreds of thousands of dollars, yet the city has never shut off their water supply. Meanwhile, residents of Detroit can lose access to water if they fall behind as little as $150 on their payments. When the water to their taps gets shut off, many are forced to buy bottled water from the very corporations that are not paying their bills in a timely fashion—forcing residents to pay 113 times more for the same water they should be getting from their sinks.

Of course, just having running water is not enough. It has to be clean. In many communities in Michigan the water supply is toxic and potentially deadly. Debt played a role there, too. In 2014, the city of Flint was operating at a $13 million deficit and was close to bankruptcy. Governor Rick Snyder's administration was hell-bent on switching Flint's water supply as a money-saving measure, but doing so would have required a new round of debt financing. Synder's administration came up with a fraudulent scheme that was a classic bait and switch. The details get complicated but a simplified version goes like this: The state of Michigan would grant Flint a special waiver allowing them to borrow more money to clean up a lime sludge lagoon, one of the many environmental disasters companies left behind when they offshored local jobs. But buried in the bond agreement was a clause requiring Flint to agree to switch its water supply as a condition for this new debt. Basically, Flint was being forced into debt to pay for its own poisoning.

The first signs that something was wrong came when Flint residents started breaking out in rashes after taking showers. Flint resident Marla Garland described it as feeling like fire ants biting all over her body that would later leave her skin itchy. "I scratched so hard I had bruises on my arms and legs." Children stopped gaining weight and stopped growing. People were losing clumps of hair. Flint water activist Lee-Ann Walters even lost her eyelashes. Things got so bad people weren't able to take showers at all, or were forced to get gym memberships out of town, shower at truck stops, or pay hotels just to take a shower. When Walters got her children's blood levels tested for lead, she broke down in tears. "I was hysterical. At first, it was self-blame. And then there's that anger: How are they letting them do this?" There is no "safe" level of lead in water, but EPA regulations require it to be under 15 parts per billion. The water coming out of Walters's tap clocked in at 400 parts per billion. Citizens of Flint, especially the children, likely face a lifetime of health risks from lead exposure, including neurological disorders and long-term organ damage.

After the switch to toxic water was made, Flint was unable to access the previous clean water supply it had been getting from Detroit—the terms of the bond agreement forbade it. *Vice News* reported that if Flint wanted clean water, "the city would be stuck with its monthly Detroit water bill and would still be on the hook for more than $100 million owed to big banks like JPMorgan Chase and Wells Fargo." Residents of Flint are still being poisoned while creditors cash in. Marginalized communities pay for financialization with their lives.

Across a range of debt types, similar troubling dynamics hold true. Households are crushed by debt and entire families suffer. In Baltimore, local hospitals have been suing former patients for past-due medical bills—people have been incarcerated and families have lost their homes as a result of one person having to go to the emergency room. Predictably, those pursued by hospital debt collectors have been disproportionately Black.

As we've seen, financialization exploits people's preexisting economic vulnerabilities. But it's important to recognize that people are emotionally exploited, too. Payday loans, for example, target single mothers who are so desperate to keep a roof over their kids' heads that they will borrow at extortionate rates. Predatory for-profit colleges like the University of Phoenix, which can be twice as expensive as Ivy League universities, play a similarly manipulative game. They spend enormous sums on advertising aimed at single mothers, Black and Latinx students, first-generation students, and veterans who want to make their families proud. A training manual for recruiters at one such school instructed its employees to "poke the pain a bit and remind them who else is depending on them and their commitment to a better future."

Here, in plain words, is another reason debtor organizing is so important. Creditors and the companies they serve are invested in the perpetuation of suffering, whether they trade in water, housing, medical care, incarceration, or education.

They'd rather "poke the pain" and profit from people's suffering than alleviate it. If we want to help our families and ourselves, we need to put these predators out of business.

UNDERSTANDING THE PAST, FIGHTING FOR A DIFFERENT FUTURE

In order to change our economic system, it helps to understand our economic history. Again and again, social movements have bravely pushed back against intergenerational forms of exclusion and prejudice and, again and again, they have had new debts imposed on them as punishment intended as a form of social control.

The Haitian Revolution, global abolition, and anticolonial movements won great victories, but they were intentionally undermined by odious debt obligations that upheld global racial hierarches—enriching some and impoverishing others—that stymied progress and destroyed lives. More than a century later, financialization continues this dynamic while adding a new twist. To those long excluded from traditional paths to economic security, financialization offered a perverse opportunity: the chance to access credit markets but under terms that benefitted lenders and collectors while, more often than not, making borrowers worse off. Government policy and corporate greed responded to demands by the women's movement and civil rights movement for inclusion in the social fabric with the "democratization" of credit, at exorbitant terms. Financialization replicates and deepens longstanding forms of inequality with new tools: variable interest rate loans and asset-backed financial products. We need to break this cycle by demanding and winning reparative public goods, not debt-financed scraps.

Because Wall Street has its tentacles everywhere in search of profit, financialization has connected us to one another at a new scale. To date, the 1 percent has leveraged those vast interconnections for profit—all of our debt interest and fee payments have been securitized, pooled, tranched, and repackaged as investable assets, moving through financial institutions across state and national borders. If we act strategically, our new web of interconnections can be transformed into a way to trap capitalists in their own net. A novel way for creditors to extract profit has opened up equally novel possibilities for debtors to get organized.

CHAPTER THREE

DEBT STRIKE
CITIES, COUNTRIES, EMPIRES

The economic system we live under is global. We buy goods made on the other side of the world. Corporations are multinational entities, operating on multiple continents simultaneously. Financial markets are open around the clock, and money crosses borders more easily than people, especially if it is denominated in US dollars. The *creditocracy*, professor Andrew Ross's term for those who benefit from financialization, wrings profit from every corner of the planet.

The scale of global capitalism means that debt doesn't just affect individuals and households. In 1945, for example, cities and towns held less than $20 billion in outstanding loans; today investors hold close to $4 trillion in what is known as municipal debt. Meanwhile, entire nations are drowning in unpayable sovereign debt. These forms of lending and borrowing help us to see how debt binds us to people we do not know, from those who live on the other side of our town to those who live on the other side of the world. Considering this reality, how might groups of debtors organize against creditors at different scales in order to push for a new economic system?

FROM HOUSEHOLDS TO CITIES

Our individual and household debts often stem from the fact that the cities we live in are broke. There's no better example of this connection than debt related to the criminal punishment system—the fines and fees imposed in courts, jails, parole relationships, and beyond. Today 2.3 million people are incarcerated in the United States; more than 35 percent of them are African American men. Between court fines, fees, and restitution payments, incarcerated people have an average of $13,607 in criminal punishment debt alone. Bail debts add exponentially to this total, effectively punishing people not for crimes but for being too poor to pay.

Making matters worse, these debts affect people's lives long after an individual has left jail or prison. The inability to make payments can subject them to re-arrest and also put their public benefits at risk. Because the failure to pay court debt is often a violation of parole or probation, individuals who can't afford to pay may be cut off from benefits such as Temporary

Assistance for Needy Families (TANF), food stamps, housing assistance, and Supplemental Security Income (SSI) for seniors and people with disabilities. Finally, in many jurisdictions, the ability to get convictions wiped off criminal records in order to access jobs or housing cannot proceed until these debts have been paid in full. Debt from the criminal punishment system drives whole families to spend years trying to dig themselves out from under mountains of bills, financially shackling people long after they've served their time.

$13,607
average criminal legal debt per incarcerated American

As we saw in the cases of Detroit and Flint in the last chapter, municipalities often need to borrow to fund basic services. In order to pay creditors, they extract as much revenue as possible from their poorest residents, which only pushes individuals and families further into debt. The result is a regressive system and a vicious cycle, where those with the least wind up paying the most.

Let's take Ferguson, Missouri, as an example of how court debt and municipal debt are produced together. In 2014, a white police officer murdered an eighteen-year-old African American man named Michael Brown. The killing sparked mass protests, brought media attention to the issue of police violence, and helped to launch the Black Lives Matter movement.

The role of court debt in the maintenance of Ferguson's extractive criminal punishment system is a critical piece of the picture. After Brown's death, the legal advocacy organization Arch City Defenders released a report noting that Ferguson, a city of just over 21,000 people, had issued almost 33,000 arrest warrants in 2013. (Yes you read that correctly, warrants outnumbered residents!) Many of these warrants were issued because people could not pay their municipal fines and fees—charges often incurred for trivial offenses such as leaving a trashcan on the street or a broken brake light. According to a class-action lawsuit (*Fant v. City of Ferguson*), the city was running a modern debtors' prison, in which impoverished people were jailed for their inability to pay court debts. The lawsuit detailed how Ferguson families were routinely compelled to use money needed for food, clothing, rent, and utilities to pay ever-increasing court fines, fees, costs, and surcharges. When they couldn't pay, they were imprisoned—something many legal experts argue is unconstitutional. Being poor shouldn't be a criminal offense.

We have to face the segregated geographies of our nation's cities if we want to understand how debt works as a form of racialized capitalist control. How did Ferguson become a segregated and hyper-policed city in the first place? In 1970, Ferguson was 99 percent white, and by 2015 it was 25 percent white. With the onset of a national recession in the '70s, investment in public services started to decline. Local municipalities in St. Louis County had to compete with each other for funds. Cities fought hard to lure businesses that, it was hoped, would create jobs and reestablish the local tax base. This strategy failed as Ferguson ended up giving land to retailers, including big box stores like Walmart, for next to nothing. Residents with means (disproportionately white) were further incentivized to move out of the city by government policy.

According to the Economic Policy Institute, segregated public housing projects replaced integrated low-income residential areas. The federal government subsidized white flight and Black marginalization. These policies were implemented during a specific moment of profound and destructive economic change. Like most of the region, Ferguson had undergone a ruthless period of deindustrialization. Then, in the 1990s under president Bill Clinton, the banking system was deregulated, and free trade agreements accelerated the destruction of industrial jobs. Ferguson lost half of its manufacturing sector during those years. To make up for its reduced tax base, the government turned to borrowing—financialization had begun. A debt crisis ensued, leading the police department to begin targeting people for arrest, in order to extract fines and fees. This was a city attempting to balance its budget on the backs and out of the pockets of criminalized African American communities.

Sadly, Ferguson is not alone. The cycle of deindustrialization, austerity, and government borrowing with no tax base to repay loans has pushed cities across the country to fund their operations, including the police and courts, by pushing those costs onto the poorest residents. Such abuses prompted professor Donna Murch to write that "the most important lesson to be learned from the brutal history of American debt peonage and convict leasing is that many of the foundations of racial inequality are economic."

After the Ferguson uprising, the US Justice Department published the *Ferguson Report*, which upbraided the city's court system for targeting residents who were the least able to pay. The report documented how city managers, police, and court personnel had conspired to extract fines and fees from people alleged to have committed minor infractions. But the report failed to emphasize the underlying economic conditions in the city. After the release of the report, which received national media attention, Moody's Investor Services dealt an economic death blow to Ferguson by downgrading its credit rating. After years of relying on the bond market to stay afloat, the municipality found itself relegated to "junk" credit status overnight. That kick in the teeth meant the city could no longer borrow to finance its daily operations. Why did Moody's make such a move against a city that had virtually no other way to survive? In explaining its decision, the company referred to the Justice Department's report. Citing the exploding costs of litigation after Michael Brown's murder and the projected legal costs after months of unrest, the agency cynically used Ferguson's racist policing practices as a pretext for cutting off essential funding.

Let's be clear about the destruction that financialization policies, developed and supported at the federal level, have wrought in one city. After Michael Brown's death, the federal government did not step in to offer new revenue to counteract the decades of disinvestment and austerity. Instead, it issued a report highlighting the city's supposedly localized abuses and recommended reforms. Wall Street then used the report as a cudgel to justify removing a critical source of revenue. In other words, entities that had helped to cause the crisis (the federal government and Wall Street) saw Brown's death not as an opportunity to rethink decades of federal and local policies that had created the intersection of racism, state violence, municipal debt, and court debt but as an invitation to berate and financially sabotage the city.

CANCEL THE DEBTS

Ferguson captured the world's attention in 2014, when protesters helped push the Black Lives Matter movement onto the national stage. Those protests changed the conversation around race and policing and also revealed how debt functions to disempower and dispossess Black communities.

The 2020 uprisings in the wake of the police murders of George Floyd, Breonna Taylor, and Ahmaud Arbery brought both household debt and municipal debt into the public conversation about systemic racism. During the Movement for Black Lives' Week of Action in June, activists called for "rent cancellation, mortgage cancellation, a moratorium on utility and water shutoffs, and cancellation of student, medical, and other forms of debt."

We need to create and support institutions that adopt these demands. What if debtors in cities like Ferguson formed a debtors' organization that could provide resources and support for collectivizing their struggles? What if such an organization could assist individuals, helping defend their legal rights, while acting as a base for taking collective action against creditors, including those collectors working on behalf of the city court system?

In a Fines and Fees debtors' union, for example, people with court debt could meet each other, face to face and online, to plan actions and campaigns specifically targeting municipal court systems, police departments, and the creditors and collectors that work for them. They could consult with lawyers, policy makers, and researchers, including those at the Action Center for Race and the Economy (ACRE), who have exposed what they call "police brutality bonds": cities and counties regularly issue

million-dollar bonds to cover the costs of police miscon-
duct, allowing banks and investors to collect fees and interests from abuse. Debtors from different parts of the city
could come together to amplify bold demands. The Debt
Free Justice California coalition has begun some of this
work and has won significant victories, including the abolition of many criminal punishment fines and fees in San
Francisco and Alameda counties.

Collective action is critical, because not even a global
pandemic is capable of curbing elected officials' commitment to stripping state and city budgets to the bone. While
bodies were piling up in refrigerated trucks outside New
York hospitals during the early days of the COVID-19 outbreak, Governor Cuomo signed a budget that rolled back
cash bail reforms, thereby condemning more poor people to
jail during a pandemic, and slashed billions from Medicaid.
"We can't spend what we don't have," he explained. As was
the case in countless communities, New Yorkers were told
there wasn't enough money for social services.

That's what we are always told. One thing debtors'
unions must do is demand a debt audit that looks into their
city's books to see if these statements are true. There is a good
chance residents are being ripped off by creditors. When cities and states need money for big projects they typically issue
bonds, borrowing to access the necessary capital. That means
our communities—including our school districts, water
and sewage systems, transportation authorities, public hospitals, and other tax-exempt debt issuers—are remarkably

dependent on Wall Street. Pension funds are a good example. For decades, states and cities have been underfunding pensions and turning those funds over to Wall Street to invest in increasingly risky and socially destructive ways, such as buying shares in Uber or betting on fossil fuels. When the economy craters, as it did in 2008, those funds lose value and teachers, nurses, firefighters, and other public retirees pay the price. In the last few years, Illinois instituted a more regressive tax system and installed parking meters to try to make up the gap in pension funding. Kentucky required schoolteachers to pay more into the system to keep it solvent, while California saw tens of billions in losses to its public pension system in the wake of the pandemic.

Banks that underwrite municipal bonds take advantage of the public's dependence on them by pushing complicated additional products that often end up costing billions in unexpected fees. One such product is known as an "interest rate swap," which can be thought of as a way for issuers of specific types of municipal bonds to hedge against rising interest rates. The problem is that if interest rates go down the bet backfires, and cities get smothered in additional debt. In 2015, in Detroit, an estimated 40 percent of all water bill payments made by cash-strapped Detroit residents went toward paying off a $547 million penalty imposed by Goldman Sachs and other banks after the city terminated interest rate swaps.

Municipal debt audits could bring deals like these into the light of day, so residents can mobilize to renegotiate the terms. By failing to adequately disclose the risks associated

with their products, some banks may be running afoul of
the law. This means cities might have both ethical and legal arguments for refusing to pay extortionate finance fees,
potentially freeing up billions that could be spent on education, infrastructure, and any number of other construc-
tive projects. In addition to informing the public about how
municipal debt really works, debt audits could pose a more
fundamental question: Why are cities being forced to borrow
money in the first place?

Part of the problem is that instead of taxing rich people
and corporations, we borrow from them, paying them interest for the privilege. Their refusal to pay taxes is a big reason state and local governments lack revenue. Changing the
equation means not just stopping budget cuts but finding new
ways to assure that cities and states have adequate financing.
Researcher Saqib Bhatti offered one suggestion in an article
about how cities might free themselves from Wall Street's control: "What if cities took a page from the labor movement and
bargained collectively over interest rates and other financial
deals?" Citing a 2012 move by the City of Oakland to boycott
Goldman Sachs over the predatory terms that plunged the
city into unpayable debt, Bhatti encourages us to think cre-
atively about how cities can build leverage against financial
entities. "American taxpayer dollars are a tremendous source
of bargaining power," he wrote. "If [a creditor] has to jump
through a few hoops to get it, it will. This gives public officials
the leverage to demand lower interest rates and fairer terms,
freeing up scarce funds for community services like parks,

libraries and schools." Bhatti is proposing something like municipal debtors' unions, organizations that would regard something that normally feels like a burden (in this case, tax and debt payments) as a potential source of collective power.

One kind of municipal union has already been tested in the UK. Inspired by the Debt Collective's work in the United States, a group called Debt Resistance UK formed in 2015. The organization exposed how banks had sold controversial loans to municipalities across the UK. The so-called "LOBO (lender option borrower option) loans" have been described by financial experts as a "lose-lose bet." Whether interest rates go up or down, municipalities always lose out. More than two hundred municipalities were sold a total of £15 billion in LOBO loans between the 1980s and 2011. The largest players were Barclays, the Royal Bank of Scotland (RBS), Dexia, and Depfa. Banks made around £1.5 billion in upfront profits from the deals, and kickbacks were flowing.

In response, Debt Resistance UK began campaigning for the cancellation of LOBO loans on the basis that they are unlawful due to both the nature of the loans and the process by which the debt was incurred. Under pressure, RBS agreed to let municipalities exit more than £1 billion of its LOBO loans with relatively low fees, with further concessions from Barclays. In the meantime, seven municipalities have taken legal action against Barclays on the basis that LOBO loans were rigged. The court cases are still underway.

Members of Debt Resistance UK set up a workers' cooperative in 2017 to continue the campaign. The cooperative,

Research for Action, is in the process of building a database
of all the loans, including the ones restructured, so that municipalities can use the data to negotiate cancellations with
the banks. Debt Resistance UK's work is one example of what
debtors can do when they band together.

GLOBAL INSURGENCIES

A financialized economy allows creditors to trap not just
individuals but entire communities in destructive debt contracts. What happened in Haiti—a small country punished
for its democratic revolution with a mountain of unpayable
debt—would become a model for others throwing off the colonial yoke more than a century later.

The power imbalance between creditor and debtor nations was further institutionalized after World War II, when
representatives from the world's largest economies gathered
to design a monetary system that would govern international
trade. As part of that process, they created the International
Monetary Fund (IMF) and the World Bank (WB), two institutions charged with lending to poor countries during
times of economic crisis. The loans were far from an act of
generosity. They were tied to strict conditions, including
a requirement that borrower nations liberalize their economies and take steps to attract foreign investment. These
"structural adjustment" programs were advertised as a way
to help poor countries build infrastructure and address poverty though they were anything but. From the point of view

of international bankers and influential politicians, they were also seen as a way to counter decolonial, democratic, and socialist ideologies, which were on the rise during the cold war. For decades, the IMF and the World Bank have coerced poor countries to prioritize debt repayment over all other considerations, including taking care of their citizens.

Communities have fought back against these odious debts, sometimes successfully. Countries in the Global South, in particular, have long led the charge against the international lending institutions that help prop up modern capitalism. In the late 1990s, for example, activists in Bolivia launched a grassroots campaign to protest the privatization of their water. The IMF had recently lent the nation $138 million for the ostensible purpose of helping to stop inflation. Buried in the loan contract was a clause that required the city of Cochabamba to sell off its public water supply. The deal also prohibited the Bolivian government from offering subsidies to help people pay their water bills, which were expected to rise exponentially with private ownership.

Cochabamba's water rights were eventually sold to an international conglomerate. In response, activists created the Coalition for the Defense of Water and Life (La Coordinadora) and organized a blockade of the city that lasted for four days. The group also launched a general strike, which spread to cities around the country. Next, La Coordinadora held an informal referendum on the water privatization plan. Ninety-six percent of those who voted said they opposed selling off their local water supply to international oligarchs. Within a few months, the movement had grown to include tens of thousands of people, including the rural Bolivians who stood to suffer the most under a privatized water system.

At first, the Bolivian government suppressed the movement. Officials declared a "state of siege" that permitted police to make arrests without charges and to detain people without warrants. Hundreds were killed and injured in the ensuing protests. Eventually, after months of unrest, the government gave in. Elected officials ultimately signed an agreement with movement leaders. They promised to rescind the water privatization legislation and to free all prisoners who had been arrested in the protests.

The Cochabamba water wars inspired protests that took place in 2000, when thousands of global justice activists descended on Washington, DC, to demand the cancellation of debts owed by poor countries. Similar protests were held around the world. Then, in 2006, leftist president Evo Morales came to power in Bolivia and institutionalized what had been a grassroots movement. He went back to Cochabamba to declare his country's total independence from the IMF and the World Bank. From now on, he said, it is "for the people to decide their destiny, the people decide their future, the people decide the hope of future generations."

The Bolivian uprising encouraged insurgencies throughout the region. By 2005, Ecuador was also in debt to international banks to the tune of $11 billion. Minister of Finance Rafael Vicente Correa decided that it wasn't right that almost

40 percent of the national budget was going to debt repayments. He argued that the money should be used instead for health care, education, and job creation programs. The World Bank announced that, if such a policy were implemented, it would halt all lending to the country. This was a dire threat, since Ecuador relied on international loans to survive. Rather than submit to the demands of lenders, though, Correa resigned from his post, an act that made him incredibly popular. Two years later, he was elected president.

While in office, Correa formed an audit committee to review fifty years of the country's debt obligations. He wanted to know which debts were legitimate and which should not be paid. The committee, which included finance experts from around the world, found that loans to Ecuador were almost always designed to benefit global corporations at the expense of ordinary people. Gail Hurley, one of the committee members, wrote about her experience auditing the country's books. Most loans, she explained,

> were to be used exclusively for the purchase of materials from the lender nation, to be assembled in-country by workers from the lender nation, with advice provided by consultants from the lender country, to be transported to Ecuador via transportation companies registered in the lender country, with repayments to be made in the currency of the lender.

In light of these findings, the committee declared most of the country's debts illegitimate. In a move that he called "life before debt," Correa announced his government would immediately stop all payments to bondholders. One of the first of its kind, Ecuador's purposeful debt default sent a signal that the region was in open revolt against international lenders. Is it any wonder that the US government and its allies have been trying to oust left wing leaders in the Global South ever since?

JUBILEE DEBT CAMPAIGN

Building on movements in Latin America, the Jubilee Debt Campaign further demonstrated that sovereign debt cancellation is possible. A coalition of European and US-based charities and nonprofit organizations, the group's goal was to pressure international lenders to cancel poor countries' debts. Their first direct action took place in Birmingham, England, where the international financial forum known as the G8 was taking place. Activists linked arms to create a human chain around the city. They demanded that international leaders cancel debts owed by the Global South to the Global North. Their chants could be heard inside the G8 meeting rooms. Over the next fifteen years, through a series of direct actions and lobbying efforts, the Jubilee Debt Campaign won $130 billion in debt relief for debtor nations.

In the wake of the COVID-19 pandemic, the campaign's work has become more important than ever. In response to the disease, enormous sums fled emerging markets while the demand for exports (on which many poor nations depend)

collapsed, guaranteeing dozens of countries would spi-
ral further into debt and default. In the context of a global
health emergency, creditor nations have been forced to acknowledge the problem. In April of 2020, a group of twenty
wealthy nations (the G20) offered to pause debt payments
from poor countries to rich ones for a few months.

In the *New York Times*, Abiy Ahmede, the prime minister of Ethiopia, argued that this was insufficient and called
for debt cancellation, pointing out that sixty-four countries
spend more on servicing their debt than they do on public
health care. Ahmede also pointed out that bilateral creditors
such as the World Bank are no longer the main source of ex-
ternal debt financing for many countries. Private-sector creditors, including investment banks and sovereign funds, hold
more and more debt. The profits of these speculators should
not be prioritized over people's survival and well-being.

That's why, along with dozens of other groups, the Jubilee Debt Campaign began demanding the outright cancellation of $1 trillion in loans. As the Director of Jubilee USA
explained, "developing countries are unprepared to deal with
the economic and health impacts of the coronavirus... Without action, tens of thousands of people will die because they
can't access life saving health services." For people in poor
nations, including those in the Global South, Rafael Correa's
term, "life or debt," is not just a slogan.

Jubilee activists have also long understood that sovereign debt is not just a financial obligation; it is a structural
impediment to national self-determination and democracy.

As coalition member Anne Pettifor noted two decades ago, poor countries that are in debt are not free. "Remove the debt," she said, "and they're no longer obliged to do what the IMF tells them." One of the Jubilee Debt Campaign's goals is the suspension of structural adjustment programs. Another is the payment of damages, meaning that rich countries owe a debt to their poorer counterparts. As one campaigner put it, "the developing countries are creditors" because "after centuries of pillage, decades of unfair trade and harmful aid conditions, and now climate injustice," they are the ones who are owed.

GREEK TRAGEDY

Sovereign debt isn't just a problem with the Global South. It is also used to dominate poorer countries in the north, including Portugal, Ireland, Spain, and Greece. The problems experienced by communities in Latin America and sub-Saharan Africa have come home to roost. Consider the example of Greece. Starting in the 1990s, European banks lent billions to the country's government so that it could import cars, medicine, oil, and warships from the north. This arrangement worked well for the corporations that were selling those products and for the banks that profited from the exchange. But it wasn't a good deal for regular people.

Still holding many of these debts, Greece joined the Eurozone in 2001, turning its monetary sovereignty over to European officials, a prerequisite for membership. When the US mortgage markets collapsed in 2008, sparking a global financial crisis, Greece needed to borrow even more to stay afloat, especially since it no longer controlled its own currency. The government ultimately took on hundreds of billions of dollars in loans from banks. Starting in 2010, in the midst of a global recession, Greece could no longer pay its debts. The International Monetary Fund and the European Union decided—incredibly—that the solution was even more borrowing. They lent Greece cash to pay off past due balances. Any individual debtor in the US who has been forced to take out a payday loan to pay a utility bill or to put gas in the car will recognize this con.

Taking out a loan to finance another loan begins a vicious cycle that never ends well for the debtor. And that is exactly what happened in Greece, where new loans were issued on the condition that the government implement austerity measures, including cutting workers' wages and pensions, raising taxes, and privatizing national assets. The number of publicly owned companies in Greece was ultimately slashed by two-thirds. Government property was put up for sale, including Greece's electricity and water supply as well as its ports. Today, these resources are the private property of international banks and rich investors.

While the banks that caused the crisis were eventually made whole, the aftermath was catastrophic for working-class Greeks. Indebted up to 175 percent of its GDP, the country was left destitute. Rates of depression, chronic health problems, suicide, and infant mortality skyrocketed. Almost half a million people, especially the young, emigrated in search of a better future.

But in this moment of dramatic upheaval, Greek people also fought back against the international creditor class that was bleeding them dry. In 2011, protesters gathered outside the Parliament to demand a public audit of the country's financial obligations, which they called a Truth Committee on Public Debt. In 2014, Syriza, a leftist political party born from the ashes of the financial crash, took power by promising healthcare, education, living wages, and other basic necessities. The president of the Greek Parliament, a member of Syriza, organized a citizens' debt audit, as protesters had demanded. The committee found that a substantial percentage of Greece's debts were illegal according to international law. This conclusion provided a judicial framework within which Greece's leaders could have refused to repay the country's debts. Organizers were hopeful that party leaders would help activists push for debt refusal at the national level.

Those hopes were quickly scuttled. Once in power, Syriza met significant roadblocks from the EU and from global banking elites. The prime minister, Alexis Tsipras, and his colleagues faced off with the European Central Bank, whose demands for austerity and privatization were brutal and uncompromising. As a bargaining chip, Tsipras called for a public referendum to ask voters to decide whether the country should allow another round of austerity. In response, the majority of Greeks answered "OXI," which means "no." The vote was a clear rejection of the politics of austerity.

Ultimately, the referendum result was ignored. Prime Minister Tsipras capitulated in the negotiations with creditors and never invoked the Truth Committee's revelations that the national debt was illegal, fearing (likely correctly) that ejection from the monetary union would spark a terrible humanitarian crisis in Greece, with retirees unable to access their pensions and hospitals having to shut their doors due to a lack of funding. Tsipras felt that he had no choice but to agree to more loans and more austerity measures. This outcome in Greece demonstrates how difficult it is to conduct an anti-austerity politics in one country when financial relationships are transnational. This is especially true in a small, relatively poor nation like Greece.

A single country can't resist global capitalism alone. That's why collective action across borders is so essential in a financialized world. The first step is recognizing that the budget rules enforced by European creditors are largely a game of smoke and mirrors. Just like the insistence by the US ruling class that the national debt means we can't afford universal health care or safe schools and functional public transit, international oligarchs maintain that sovereign debts must be paid on the backs of workers, students, and pensioners. They are wrong.

Once in a while the powerful admit that the economic edicts they usually enforce can be broken. During the COVID-19 pandemic, for example, the European Union suspended limits on deficit spending to enable states to boost their capacity to beat back the virus. Temporarily loosening the constraints on local economies was just the beginning.

In the spring of 2020, EU finance ministers also announced their own massive stimulus in the form of debt repayment holidays and new loans to member states. According to former Syriza party member Costas Lapavitsas, "the [COVID-19] crisis has forced the EU to engage in economic policy that side-steps its own rule book," which makes you wonder why those rules existed in the first place.

PUERTO RICO'S FIGHT FOR THE FUTURE

Puerto Rico is part of the United States, but it is not a state. It is an "unincorporated US territory." Residents can vote in the presidential election but they have no representatives in Congress. They are second-class citizens. US empire is a fundamental part of the global capitalist system.

The island has long been treated as exploitable and expendable. For decades, the colony was the site of a US military base on the island of Vieques. Starting in the 1940s, naval vessels and planes conducted training missions off the coast. In 1998 alone, 23,000 bombs were dropped on the island and live training operations took place 180 days out of the year. In the process, tons of chemicals, including mercury and lead, were dumped in the area, turning Vieques into one of the most toxic places in the Caribbean. Over the years, the site was a frequent target of protests by locals, 50 percent of whom, on average, were unemployed. The US government refused to acknowledge that its activities were harmful until 1999, when two navy jets misfired their weapons. A security guard named David Sanes Rodriguez was killed when a five-hundred-pound bomb dropped on his head. In the aftermath of the accident, the military made plans to depart, finally leaving the island in 2003. Vieques residents have not recovered. They are still struggling with above-average rates of illnesses such as hypertension, asthma, and other respiratory ailments. After decades of munitions dumps, the island was finally named an EPA Superfund site in 2005.

A few years later, another US-created disaster, one that would also have implications for the environment, hit Puerto Rico. This time, it was a debt crisis provoked by the 2008 housing market collapse. As a global recession landed on its shores, Puerto Rico turned to borrowing to stay afloat. The government began issuing tax-exempt bonds, meaning that the investors who bought them would not have to pay taxes on their profits. With the help of (surprise, surprise) Goldman Sachs, officials also issued "capital appreciation bonds" in which the rate of repayment increases over time. Those payments go mostly to covering the interest (which can be up to 1000 percent), so payments increase, but the total amount owed never goes down.

As early as 2009, the island was in deep financial trouble. As with Greece a few years later, the government imposed austerity measures, laying off seventeen thousand public sector workers and cutting pensions and public services. Predictably, austerity exacerbated the problem. By 2015, debt payments had quintupled. The next year, the US Congress passed the PROMESA law, which put Puerto Rico under the authority of a body known as the Financial Oversight and Management Board. The seven board members, appointed by the US president, were charged with assuring that the colony's assets were sold off to pay its debts.

Puerto Ricans did not take this predation and abuse without a fight. Activists had already been working to wean the island off its dependence on foreign imports of fuel and food. Local farmers were setting up infrastructure to grow more crops and, in collaboration with academics, activists were developing sustainable energy systems. One environmentalist, Alexis Massol-González, told author Naomi Klein that Puerto Ricans planned to "adopt a solar energy system and leave behind oil, natural gas, and carbon." Such a transformation would keep resources and jobs in the community.

The movement against debt peonage and for local control of the island's resources was also taking place in the streets. According to Klein, by 2016, "a popular movement calling for an independent audit of the debt was quickly gaining ground, spurred by the conviction that if its causes were closely examined, as much as 60 percent of the more than $70 billion Puerto Rico supposedly owe[d] would be found to have been accumulated in violation of the island's constitution." This news helped to push students at the University of Puerto Rico to go on strike to protest tuition hikes and budget cuts. Then, on May 1, 2016, more than a hundred thousand people flooded into the streets of San Juan to protest austerity and demand an audit of the colony's debt.

It looked like this popular revolt might mount a challenge to creditors, forcing them to negotiate down the debt. Then, in 2017, Hurricane Maria crashed into the island, killing more than three thousand people and destroying up to 80 percent of the local food crops. The protest movement was disrupted as residents spent the next few years rebuilding their homes and preparing to reopen their businesses and schools. Rolling blackouts as well as food and water shortages were exacerbated by a series of earthquakes that struck in 2020. Calls to suicide hotlines skyrocketed as people struggled to recover.

With so many desperate just to survive, the protest movement was dampened and activists had to regroup. "With the status quo so untenable," Klein explained, "anything at all can seem like an improvement." The colony's creditors could hardly have hoped for a better outcome. Entrepreneurs from the US mainland also descended on the island to take advantage of the crisis. The local government rolled out the red carpet, inviting business owners to move their companies to avoid US taxes. (A clause in the US tax code allows companies technically based in Puerto Rico to pay a fraction of what they would be charged on the mainland.) The combined offer of low regulation and low taxes proved irresistible to corporate executives who needed a place to stash their cash. One entrepreneur, newly arrived from California, was caught on film imagining Puerto Rico as the next Silicon Valley. "If Puerto Rico creates an environment where government services are privatized, we can start encouraging entrepreneurs to start businesses," he said. "Twenty thousand [government employees] are cops. We need the cops. But pretty much everything else should be privatized." In the aftermath of a hurricane that had killed thousands and destroyed much of the island's infrastructure, US companies saw a vast terrain of resources to be mined and extracted while government-funded police patrolled the streets.

An economic crisis followed by an environmental disaster has set the stage for the further financialization of Puerto Rico by plutocrats bent on privatizing public services. This scenario raises a question that is central to the Debt Collective's organizing work and to this book: *Who owes what to whom?* Puerto Ricans may be in debt according to the normal rules of capitalism, but after more than a hundred years of colonialism, decades of predatory lending by banks, and a capitalism-induced climate crisis, it is clear that *ordinary Puerto Ricans are the ones who are owed.* In Puerto Rico, where the struggle against creditors is also a battle between the victims of climate change and its profiteers, a debtors' movement was underway before Hurricane Maria struck. International cooperation is what is needed to help see such a movement through.

DEBTORS ACROSS BORDERS

In the age of financialization, popular uprisings have become increasingly common. Poor people's protest movements exploded around the globe in 2019. In Chile, the country many consider the birthplace of neoliberalism, an increase in subway fares sparked weeks of demonstrations. Protesters demanded an end to low wages, to mass indebtedness, and to the decades-long looting of their country by foreign capitalists. Their anger has a long history. In the 1970s, Chile was the site of a brutal military coup that installed a US-backed dictator, who introduced a series of dramatic free-market reforms.

In Ecuador, indigenous people and students protested a $4.2 billion loan from the International Monetary Fund, along with higher fuel prices. The demonstrations resulted in violent repression, leaving seven dead and hundreds injured. Haiti, the poorest country in the Western Hemisphere, has also been the site of a popular revolt. After their US-backed president tried to end fuel subsidies at the bidding of the IMF, Haitians rose up to demand his resignation. They have also accused government officials of stealing billions in aid that flowed into the country after the 2010 earthquake.

On the other side of the globe, in Lebanon, demonstrations broke out in October 2019 after the government announced it would impose higher taxes in order to cut the deficit. Protesters flowed into the streets to denounce government corruption and to demand a complete overhaul of the political system. European leaders have not been spared the outrage of ordinary people. In France, the so-called Yellow Vests brought the country to a halt as demonstrators protested the high cost of living amid tax breaks for the rich. The police cracked down on the movement. Hundreds were injured, including at least two dozen people whose eyes were blinded by police using rubber bullets. The Yellow Vests were not deterred. Fed up with condescending leaders whose deeds did not match their rhetoric, they rallied at first under a slogan that pitted environmental sustainability against day-to-day survival: "The elites talk about the end of the world while we are talking about the end of the month." Demonstrators soon adopted a different, more collective motto: "End of the world, end of the month, same struggle."

Debtors' unions could help connect the need for an economic system that does not destroy our environment to the need for basic social protections for ordinary people. International organizing to change the power dynamic between debtors and creditors will be difficult. But, after the pandemic, it is more obvious than ever that it is necessary. The Coronavirus crisis helped to expose that EU budget rules, for example, were always a political choice. Unfortunately, that revelation will not stop creditors from returning to a politics of punishment. Before most countries had beaten back the virus, an IMF spokesperson was quoted in the *Financial Times*: "Once economies recover," he said, "achieving progress on ensuring debt sustainability will be needed." In other words, once the crisis passes, debtor nations should prepare to be beaten into submission (again) by lenders. This scenario is especially troubling, considering environmental disasters are likely to increase in the years to come. As Kate Aronoff wrote in the *Guardian*, "If normal was bad for low-income countries before, it won't get better as seas rise." The feeling of being coerced into a debt that can't be repaid and then having austerity measures forced on you is certainly something to which many individual debtors can relate.

As the pandemic continues to threaten lives and livelihoods, researchers have projected that massive shortfalls to
state and local budgets are on the way. With already under-
funded public services like education and healthcare on the
chopping block, more of us will have no choice but to take
on debt to meet our basic needs. The situation looks even
more dire when we consider that, in cities such as New York
and Los Angeles, police department budgets were swiftly ex-
empted from potential cuts. In some cases, they have been
issued additional funds so that cops can work overtime, policing increasingly desperate populations. Many people in
other nations have long had to live under the threat of the US
military. Now, more and more, residents of the US are facing
down militarized police forces that are armed with weapons
developed for killing in war zones. Yet vital public services
continue to be starved of revenue.

These connections between individual struggles, national financial crises, and global events must be identified,
magnified, and cultivated as sites of collective struggle. Imagine international debtors' assemblies where all kinds of people—working-class people and their allies—meet in person
and online to share experiences and work together to discuss
what a more equitable distribution of global resources might
look like. Indeed, it is not top-down educational initiatives
or paternalistic lecturing that turns isolated individuals into
political actors; it is thinking and acting with others toward
concrete, achievable goals. Conversations about economics are usually conducted by professionals or technocratic

elites, using obscure terminology and in forums seemingly intended to exclude regular people. We insist that broad, democratic engagement on such critical questions as capitalism, globalization, and credit markets must be conducted by debtors themselves in organizations set up and funded for that purpose. This is a role that debtors' unions can play.

We have been a part of these conversations ourselves. As debtors trying to get organized, it took us a few years to understand our own debts as collectively held, rather than as individual liabilities. And when former Corinthian College students began making demands for debt relief, most of them regarded their problems as individual as well. They believed they had attended an outlier scam school. They believed that they had been wronged in particular ways with consequences that affected them alone. As organized debt strikers, however, former students met with people who had attended other predatory schools and heard stories similar to their own. They also began hearing from student debtors more broadly. It turned out that even people who had attended traditional colleges were drowning in debt. As the strikers' circle of comrades expanded, so did their vision of a world where public goods—including education—are available to all. This is one reason that movement building—the act of sharing our struggles and deciding what to do about them together—is so crucial.

Learning can serve as a springboard to action. When we talk about Greece's creditors and the collectors that harass US debtors, for example, we are often talking about the same institutions. Goldman Sachs, for instance, profited hand-somely from Greece's financial crisis. It lent money to the country in the lead-up to the crash, enriching investors in the process. After the US mortgage market meltdown, ordi-nary Greeks, who were struggling to keep medicine in stock and food on the shelves, watched while Goldman Sachs, along with other Wall Street banks, got bailed out to the tune of trillions of dollars. In subsequent years, US debtors watched similar phenomena unfold. Not only did the De-troit Water Department pay $547 million to terminate usu-rious loans, Oakland, California, also found itself trapped in an interest-rate swap engineered by Goldman Sachs, for which it had to pay a $16 million exit fee. Though we may live in different countries, inhabit unique cultures, speak differ-ent languages, when it comes to our status as debtors, the institutions that exploit us are one and the same. The goal of any debtors' union should be to help us to see ourselves as in the same boat—and in the same struggle—as our fellow debtors across the sea.

CHAPTER FOUR

DISRUPTING DYSTOPIA
ALGORITHMIC EXTRACTION
AND DIGITAL REDLINING

D ebtors' unions are possible—and scalable. We are connected across households, cities, and countries by our debts to rapacious, imperialist financial institutions. We can use those connections to take power and remake our economic system. If we are in a moment of finance capitalism, we are also increasingly in a moment of what Shoshanna Zuboff calls "surveillance capitalism," a system based on the violation of our privacy and exploitation of our data. Big Tech is the latest incarnation of capitalist colonialism, a virtual engine of dispossession and enclosure that spans the globe.

We need to stop and analyze the future we are racing toward. What new forms of extraction and domination are being developed? What new forms of solidarity and collective action does digitization make possible, so we can redesign the economy? The fight for a different digital world is already underway, and debtors need to join it.

As things stand, digitization is too often a tool of financialization and extraction. It is a Trojan horse that allows venture capitalists, corporate executives, and state officials to paint old-fashioned deregulation and profit-seeking as novel and "innovative." Austerity is hidden behind, and advanced by, invisible and unaccountable algorithms. Automation is employed to speed up and degrade work, as well as to pay workers lower wages, often far less than minimum wage. Payday loans are rebranded through "fintech," short for financial technology, that allows fees and interest to accrue with the swipe of a screen. Wireless technologies enable autolenders to remotely disable vehicles if a borrower falls behind on monthly payments (this has even happened while people are driving down the road, endangering their lives). The internet facilitates the accumulation of wealth and privatization of our personal information on a previously unimaginable scale, funneling the vast majority of the rewards to a handful of American robber barons and their shareholders.

The stakes could not be higher for those of us who are not running the show. Automated systems are increasingly tasked with life and death determinations: who qualifies for welfare services, who gets watched or arrested by the police, who is a friend or foe (the state does not know the identities of 75 percent of people killed by drones, but we do know that 20 percent of them were women and children), and who has a chance to immigrate. In 2018 we learned that the risk-assessment software used by Immigration and Customs Enforcement (ICE) agents was altered to yield only one outcome: the system recommended "detain" and not "release" for 100 percent of immigrants in custody. If digital and algorithmic systems are discriminatory, they are this way by design, perpetuating inequality without public debate or consent. "Weapons of math destruction," as technologist Cathy O'Neill calls them; "algorithms of oppression," in the words of scholar Safiya Noble.

As COVID-19 swept the country and millions of people lost their jobs, we saw just how dependent we are on a handful of giant tech companies, and how dangerous this dependence is. Jeff Bezos, founder of Amazon and the richest man on earth, added $24 billion and counting to his fortune in the early weeks of the outbreak. The workers he employed weren't so lucky. News reports revealed that managers at Whole Foods, a company Amazon had recently acquired, were tracking workers with a high-tech "heat map" to preempt any attempts to form a union. It wasn't a novel approach—finance firms and banks had been using machine-learning programs to monitor worker sentiment well before the pandemic.

Silicon Valley, as we'll see, has a habit of emulating Wall Street. The two sectors have more in common than we're typically led to believe, and they are merging in alarming ways. Debtors' unions can and must pay attention to these new developments, so we can confront them head on.

BROKE ON PURPOSE

In early 2020, while Bezos was raking in the cash, government websites across America were crashing. It wasn't that previously functional systems were flooded with claimants they weren't prepared to handle. In Florida, former governor Rick Scott had purposely designed the online system to make it hard for people to access aid. "It's a sh-- sandwich, and it was designed that way by Scott," said one of his former advisors. "It wasn't about saving money. It was about making it harder for people to get benefits or keep benefits so that the unemployment numbers were low to give the governor something to brag about." When hundreds of thousands of people needed help, the state's online system made it effectively impossible for them to even apply.

The Debt Collective has been undermined by exactly this sort of strategy. When we started to make use of the right called "borrower defense to repayment" (which allows students to petition to get their debts discharged when their schools violate the law to put them in debt), we created an online form that would make the process as simple and user friendly as possible. After thousands of people used the Debt Collective's tool to assert their rights and get debt relief, the Department of Education announced that all future claims would have to be made directly through the government's official website. On Secretary DeVos's watch, a new ninety-million-dollar redesign was ordered, only to be scrapped. In 2020 a whistleblower within the Department of

Education revealed that the redesign was rejected by Diane Auer Jones, a political appointee, because it provided borrowers with too much information and was too user friendly. To prevent debtors from exercising their rights, the Department of Education deliberately made the process as confusing and difficult as possible. The Debt Collective was able to make the process simple and clear with a tiny fraction of the budget, and was sabotaged for doing so.

Around the world, technology is employed to cut costs, shrink public services, and disempower and demoralize anyone who needs assistance. In Michigan, governor Rick Snyder, the same guy who is responsible for poisoning the water in Flint, created a $46 million dollar automated fraud detection algorithm, powered by artificial intelligence, that falsely accused tens of thousands of people, automatically garnishing their wages and seizing their tax refunds and social security payments as penalties for crimes they did not commit. Many people ended up losing their homes or were forced into greater debt because their salaries were being stolen from them. The fraud detection system had a 93 percent error rate, and those errors impacted more than forty thousand people. Because the whole system was automated, there was no human they could call, no paperwork they could file, no office they could visit in order to correct the error and get their money back.

These malfunctions did not emerge in a vacuum. There is a long, disturbing precedent for this misuse of technology. The state first began to adopt digital tools as part of a concerted conservative backlash to erode progressive gains. It began as a strategy to undermine women-led social movements that were successfully demanding more from the state, including less degrading forms of public benefits.

In the late sixties and early seventies, during the Great Society period, the national welfare rights movement saw extraordinary success, including numerous legal victories: it became illegal to discriminate against people receiving Aid to Families with Dependent Children (AFDC); due process rights for welfare recipients were enshrined in law; and the "man-in-house" rules that allowed caseworkers to raid the homes of poor women to look for evidence of male cohabitants were scuttled. Virginia Eubanks, in *Automating Inequality*, explains how new digital tools were adopted to undercut these progressive victories, and it worked. Under the guise of increasing "efficiency," computerization began to be employed to detect fraud and tighten eligibility rules. "That's when they started culling the rolls—using these technical means," Eubanks told an interviewer. In 1973, almost 50 percent of people living under the poverty line were receiving some kind of cash assistance. Now it's less than 10 percent.

Bureaucracy is often thought of as "faceless," where humans are reduced to paperwork or numbers, but in the past there has always been a person somewhere, buried under the mountain of paperwork. Technology has eliminated those jobs or forced human caseworkers to behave more like heartless robots. Along with stigmatizing welfare recipients, the government began more closely scrutinizing caseworkers, "cutting down on their discretion," Eubanks recounts. "As surveillance of recipients increased, so did surveillance of frontline workers. They introduced much more punitive processes, with much less human connection. And that also has continued in the systems we see today." Digital bureaucracy is faceless in a new way. There is no human to speak to at any step of the process, no one capable of looking past the paperwork and seeing another human being with compassion. Making us feel alone, helpless, and frustrated is precisely the point. Meanwhile, the lack of access to social services pushes people further into debt.

OUR DATA, THEIR PROFIT

Each one of us is an invaluable person related to innumerable others through family, community, work, friendship. And yet powerful interests envision a future in which we are nothing but numbers fed into the cloud, spread across the internet's servers. We leave a trail of data online, yet we are unable to access it or use it to advance the common good. Instead, this collectively produced resource—our information—is used to help a handful of corporate giants further accumulate private gain and ward off socialized alternatives.

Silicon Valley's primary business model is surveillance. The sector has made it virtually impossible for individuals to opt out of being tracked, which is why we need to fight back en masse—the survivalist approach of individually wrapping ourselves in cloaks of encryption cannot lead to structural change. Online and offline, a range of invasive technologies track our movements. Every click is tracked and monitored, analyzed, and repackaged as an asset; every comment and purchase logged and recorded; every turn we make using GPS stored. "A couple of decades ago, letting a company read your mail and observe your social interactions and track your location would strike many, if not most, as a breach of privacy," writes technology critic Ben Tarnoff. "Today, these are standard, even banal, aspects of using the internet. It's worth considering what further concessions will come to feel normal in the next 20 years, as Silicon Valley is forced to dig deeper into our lives for data."

Predictive analytics is all about social control and securing profit, not giving us what we want or making us safer, as techno-boosters insist. The goal is to rank and rate us, so companies can score us and maximize revenue. What are your tastes? Who do you associate with in real life or on social media? What do you post about and search for? All these choices matter. This isn't some imaginary dystopian future or something that only happens in far-off authoritarian states. Online personalization and targeted marketing mechanisms are already here and becoming more and more ubiquitous.

These developments have tremendous implications for debtors, who have long been subjected to a vice grip of surveillance. Private companies with cool Silicon Valley–sounding names like Sift, Riskified, Zeta Global, Retail Equation, and Kustomer track everything from private messages sent via social media, to records of purchases, all to try to assess how "trustworthy" you are. Insurance companies are getting in on the game, mining health data to determine risk, charging people different rates based on preexisting conditions or lifestyle—not as reported to a doctor, but based on behavior and messages on social media and the internet more broadly. (Think twice before you Google "ovarian cancer.") Armed with this intel, companies are rolling out "dynamic" pricing, which is just a catchy name for price discrimination. Based on your past activity and purchases they know that you really love this particular thing and will likely pay more for it than your neighbor, so you get charged more than they do. The same will go for interest rates of lines of credit and mortgages. You'll be charged more for the money you borrow, but you won't know you are being gouged—and you certainly won't know why.

In a data-driven personalized world, we have no way to know how others are being treated online, or what is being kept out of our sights. Older white men on social media may be shown listings for high-paying jobs, while younger Black social media users might get "sponsored content" aiming to dissuade them from voting, while affluent Asian youth are targeted with pitches for a summer music festival. One person sees an ad for an American Express Gold Card, another for an extortionate payday loan.

Proving you've been discriminated against by digital decision-making systems is notoriously difficult, even when it is technically illegal. How can you tell if you're being targeted with an advertisement for an inferior or bogus financial product because data brokers have deemed you part of the "rural and barely making it," "probably bipolar," or "gullible elderly" market segments? (Yes, those are real categories advertisers use.) Or if you're being offered a jacked-up interest or insurance rate based on your race, gender, neighborhood, or health condition? Or whether you're receiving offers for a subprime financial product because a marketing score flags you as a risk? The answer is, you can't. Creditors have long aimed to keep debtors in the dark—and digital technology makes it much easier for them to do so.

FROM JIM CROW TO JIM CODE

We are taught early on to worry about our credit scores. Everyone knows the three big credit reporting agencies—Experian, Equifax, and TransUnion—that manage error-riddled dossiers on every one of us. The numbers they give us can determine our fate. Whether we can rent an apartment, be approved for a mortgage, or get a job can hang in the balance. The insidious notion that our credit history speaks to our trustworthiness as human beings must be challenged. The system currently in place is defective, punitive, and costly—some estimate that a low credit score can cost individuals hundreds of thousands of dollars over the course of their lifetimes. It is also prejudiced.

Credit scores have long been shown to perpetuate racial disparities in wealth and financial security, since individuals with lower scores are locked out of opportunity, charged higher interest rates, and driven deeper into debt. They exacerbate inequality in other ways too. For example, in the United

States it is illegal to discriminate in hiring based on the color of your skin, but it is perfectly legal to discriminate based on credit scores—a loophole companies are eager to take advantage of. It just so happens that skin color and credit information often correlate—Black people live more economically precarious lives due to structural racism and are targeted by financial predators, which leads to ruined scores—allowing a seemingly innocuous number to serve as a proxy for race in highly damaging and arguably illegal ways.

Our current credit scoring system is a disaster that needs to be overhauled. Unfortunately, things only get worse online. Tech companies turn our digital activities into "consumer" or "marketing" scores that are ingeniously devised to bypass existing (and woefully inadequate) consumer protection laws. The algorithms behind these scores are designed to predict spending—whether prospective customers will be moneymakers or money-losers. While federal law limits the use of traditional credit scores and dictates that people must be notified when an adverse decision is made about them, the law does not cover the new digital evaluation systems: You are not legally entitled to see your marketing score, let alone ensure its accuracy. In reality, there's no reason longstanding consumer protections shouldn't apply to the digital landscape. But by putting old forms of privacy-violating, discriminatory, predatory behavior into new shiny packaging, Big Tech has convinced regulators to look the other way.

The use of data-driven methods for judging people's creditworthiness goes back a century. Before the passage of the Fair

Credit Reporting Act (FCRA) in 1970, consumer-reporting bureaus would gather information on everything they could find about people—whether true or fabricated, relevant or irrelevant—and provide it to creditors. Your dossier was likely to contain whatever information they could get away with collecting or making up about you. So, if you were considered a sexual deviant, a drunk, a troublemaker, an adulterer, or anything else, it was all fair game if a creditor was willing to pay for that information. The FCRA was meant to limit these practices by putting an end to the collection of "irrelevant" information and establishing rules for the "permissible" uses of consumer reports. In 1974, Congress passed the Equal Credit Opportunity Act, which added more bite to financial regulations by making it illegal for creditors to discriminate against applicants on the basis of race, religion, national origin, sex, marital status, age, or receiving public assistance. Of course discrimination still occurs—just look at what happened leading up to the 2008 mortgage crisis—but it's technically against the law. Now even these inadequate protections are being "disrupted" in the name of innovation.

These profound flaws make it all the more outrageous that credit scores and consumer reports can have immense consequences for our lives. The lack of a score—or a low score—can mean higher interest rates within the mainstream banking system. Or it can mean being forced into the arms of check-cashing services and payday lenders. Scores can become "self-fulfilling prophecies, creating the financial distress they claim merely to indicate," legal scholars

Danielle Citron and Frank Pasquale observe. The worse your score, the more you're charged—and the more you're charged, the harder it is to make monthly payments, which means the worse you're ranked the next time around, putting you on the path to being a revolver, which is of course what lenders want all borrowers to be. (Greece is a revolver. Puerto Rico is a revolver. We are all potential revolvers.)

With the sheer quantity of data that can be collected online, FICO scores (named for the Fair Isaac Corporation) are just the tip of the credit scoring iceberg. The system has exploded thanks to the emergence of all sorts of actors that you don't actually have a direct relationship with: network advertisers, data brokers, and other sundry companies busy vacuuming up information. This information comes from online and off-line sources: thousands of data brokers keep tabs on everything from social-media profiles and online searches to public records and retail loyalty cards. They likely know things including (but not limited to) your age, race, gender, and income; who your friends are; whether you're ill, looking for a job, getting married, having a baby, or trying to buy a home. Much of the information collected is as irrelevant and prejudiced as the hearsay assembled during the early days of consumer reporting, and we have no way of knowing how it's being weighted or why it matters. Auto insurers can, for example, collect data from a device in your vehicle; this data, because it isn't acquired through a third party, isn't covered by the FCRA, and consumers have no right to access, understand, or correct the information or assessment.

The opacity and unaccountability of online consumer-credit scoring and personalized data tracking and targeting doesn't just negatively affect individuals—who might, say, be charged more for insurance or a higher interest rate on a loan. It has pernicious social effects. For example, there is evidence that these practices played a role in the subprime-mortgage bubble and subsequent financial crisis. "From 2005 to 2007, the height of the boom in the United States, mortgage and financial-services companies were among the top spenders for online ads," a scholarly article on digital decision-making and the FCRA reports. Companies like Google, Yahoo, Facebook, and Bing make billions a year from online financial marketing. Lead generation, specifically, "played a critical, but largely invisible, role in the recent subprime-mortgage debacle." (Lead generation is a multibillion-dollar industry devoted to compiling and selling lists of prospective customers.) Since 2008, when the housing crash occurred, the capabilities for tracking and targeting have become only more sophisticated.

Welcome to the age of digital redlining. The term conjures the period when banks drew red lines on actual maps to guide them in discriminating against residents of particular neighborhoods. Today, invisible algorithms exclude on lenders' behalf. "Just as neighborhoods can serve as a proxy for racial or ethnic identity, there are new worries that big data technologies could be used to 'digitally redline' unwanted groups, either as customers, employees, tenants, or recipients of credit," a 2014 White House report on Big Data warns. Unsurprisingly, Democrats in the Obama administration, eager to court deep-pocketed venture capitalists and Silicon Valley CEOs, did nothing to rein in the problem when they had the chance. In fact, many high-profile Obama staffers rushed to work with Silicon Valley as soon as they left the public sector, including former campaign manager turned Uber executive David Plouffe and former attorney general Eric Holder, who went to Airbnb before joining the Chan Zuckerberg Initiative.

The Chan Zuckerberg Initiative is, of course, the notorious Facebook founder's philanthropic arm. We can be certain that a substantial portion of Mark Zuckerberg's astonishing fortune came from his policy of permitting discriminatory advertisements on his platform. In 2016, a *ProPublica* investigation revealed that Facebook was allowing landlords to prevent "ethnic affinity" groups from seeing their ads, in clear violation of the Fair Housing Act and other laws. A year later, they were still excluding "African-Americans, mothers of high school students, Spanish speakers, and people interested in wheelchair ramps" from seeing rental ads.

Automated decision-making has not eliminated the bias baked into our economic system; rather it has enshrined socioeconomic disparities in a technical process. Racism is encoded in bad data sets and reinforced by the biases of the disproportionately white, male, and privileged engineers designing the systems we now depend on—a process scholar Ruha Benjamin calls the "New Jim Code." One recent study found that, among online mortgage applicants, Black and Latinx borrowers paid over 5 basis points more in interest than non-minority borrowers with similar financial backgrounds.

In response to such revelations, the Trump administration's Department of Housing and Urban Development proposed new rules pertaining to automated discrimination in the housing market, effectively exempting technologies from civil rights regulations and allowing algorithms to exclude and segregate on a landlord or mortgage lender's behalf. "It's going to drive people toward these algorithmic tools, and I think we'll end up in a marketplace where everyone is taking advantage of this loophole," Paul Goodman, a housing justice advocate, told *Dissent*. Lenders will be able to legally charge extortionate rates or deny people credit based on race, as long as a bot can be blamed.

THE FINTECH FUTURE

In 2014 JP Morgan Chase CEO Jamie Dimon published his annual letter to shareholders and warned that Silicon Valley was coming to eat Wall Street's lunch. That tech companies were looking to the financial sector to figure out their next move was hardly shocking—in many ways Wall Street had inspired their current business model. Old-fashioned financial institutions made early investments in data mining and analysis, paving the way for surveillance capitalism. For decades, credit card companies have used our purchases to create complex psychological portraits of us—profiles that can both be used by sales agents to push products we don't need and also by debt collectors to manipulate us into paying up. Silicon Valley didn't innovate the technique of spying on customers, they just perfected it.

But they have reached a wall. The constraints of the real world mean there is finite growth for their current regime—there are only so many human beings on the planet to bring online and show ads to. Tech companies will need to find new ways to monetize their user base, and offering financial services is one promising source of growth. This is why Uber, for example, has announced Uber Money—they want to be a driver's employer and their payday lender and their subprime auto dealer. Following in Facebook's footsteps, Walmart recently filed a patent application to create its own cryptocurrency, and Amazon is targeting its less creditworthy customers with a subprime credit card, which has higher rates and can be used only on its platforms. In 2019 Apple Card, a partnership with Goldman Sachs, was immediately revealed to be riddled with gender bias—women's applications were denied even when they had better credit scores than men, and husbands were offered ten times the credit limit of their wives. We are on the brink of a paradigm that combines the tech sector's vast data grab, proprietary algorithms, and direct personalization with the financial sector's avarice and access to federal support programs, which came in handy in 2008 and 2020 when they got bailed out with public money. Two of the biggest and greediest sectors on earth—technology and finance—are looking for ways to join forces.

As often happens, the Global South has been a laboratory for these kinds of dystopian experiments. In Kenya, a variety of mobile lending apps trap users in a cycle of debt, with people borrowing from one app to pay off loans from another. Kenya, called Africa's "Silicon Savannah," is enabled by a state that offers few safeguards, in addition to a population desperate for money that can be used to survive the day, to buy food or cooking fuel. The apps employ constant messaging and "nudging," pushing people to borrow more than they can afford and shaming them for not paying on time. "It is also a cycle of indebtedness which the lenders have little incentive to break," one report explains. "While borrowers scramble to repay, fintech firms have structured the market to benefit from iterative borrowing." Each time a loan is taken out, more user data is harvested, and fixed percentage facilitation fees mean a boost in corporate profits. It is what Professor Ananya Roy calls poverty capital, gone digital.

The effects are long-term. In Kenya, it costs twenty US dollars, a very substantial sum by local standards, to dispute one's credit score, which means a growing number of people are stuck being blacklisted, locked out of less predatory lending systems and formal employment options. Lending companies, backed by US investors, are profiting handsomely off of poor people's debt, data, and desperation. This isn't "financial inclusion," it's predatory extraction.

DATA FOR THE PEOPLE

What do tech companies, oil companies, and finance companies all have in common? They are all extractive.

Platforms such as Facebook and Google span the globe, harvesting data from our everyday activities—emails to

friends and family, checking the weather, a scan of the head-
lines—and privatize what should be a virtual commons,
something we all hold together. Fossil fuel companies dig up
hydrocarbons, our shared inheritance, from deep within the
earth. They have pursued their destructive business model
despite knowing for decades that the fate of life on this planet
hangs in the balance. Finance companies, vampire-squid
like, suck money from all aspects of our lives, skimming fees
and raking in record profits by charging what is effectively a
private tax on almost every purchase we make.

For this privilege, these are the most enormously valued
sectors on earth. With a license to extract revenue from every corner of social life, these companies have amassed hundreds of billions of dollars. And what do they do with these
mountains of cash? They hoard it, funnel it into real estate or
financial markets, or buy up competitors in a quest for market dominance and monopoly control. Their power to determine investment is arguably the most antidemocratic aspect
of this entire charade. Money flows to start-ups like Uber
and Lyft, to fund fossil fuel pipeline construction, and to en-
gineer predatory lending apps instead of improving public
transit, building solar grids and wind farms, or raising working people's wages. At the global level, between 2005 and
2019, investment growth fell from 5.7 percent to 1.6 percent.
Tech companies like Apple would rather sit on their assets or
devise new forms of planned obsolescence than invest in the
things we all need to survive and thrive: renewable energy,
social housing, education, transit, and health care.

It shouldn't be that way. That money is ours—it comes from the earth and from everyone's labor, digital and otherwise. We should not only share in the proceeds but have a say over how it is spent. To rationally allocate capital, to invest it in the things we need to survive and thrive from sustainable energy to quality housing and healthcare for everyone, we need to move beyond capitalism.

Nowhere is this more obvious than in the digital realm. Online, user data is the ultimate commodity—the thing bought and sold to make a profit. But who makes that commodity? We do, when we use social media or do anything involving the internet. Are we paid for that? No. Our unpaid digital labor generates unimaginable economic value, a situation some critics have described as "digital serfdom." Our unpaid work under digital capitalism reminds us of how important unpaid labor has been over the entire history of our messed up economic system, whether it's enslaved labor of Africans and their descendants, the unpaid labor of women in the household to reproduce workers for capitalists—or us, the digital housewives of the internet—unwittingly providing value to the tech patriarchy. Tech's wealth results from the combined contributions of *billions* of people, living and dead—and yet the resulting wealth and power accrue to a handful of billionaires.

The data being produced belongs to all of us, not just the few who are positioned to capture and privatize it. We need to create an infrastructure and economic relationships that honor this basic reality. We need to pull the plug on the subsidies that sustain the extractive class, disrupt Silicon Valley's antisocial business models, and reclaim our shared resources for the public good. Debtors must play a role in that fight. The first step is going far beyond the limited frame of "consumer protections," which inevitably leads to individualized solutions to systemic failures. Debtors know all too well how inadequate these safeguards are—predatory lending and abuse have continued despite the protections we have on the books. Instead of limited protections we must begin to think in terms of public ownership and benefit.

Today we are constantly told that we have only two options, that we must give our power and freedom over to the state, because it is the only thing that can protect us from the unregulated horrors of private industry, or that we must acquiesce to private corporations because they are the only thing that can beat back the authoritarian state. But this is a false choice. We don't have to choose between something like the infamous Chinese social credit system or a Big Tech autocracy overseen by Mark Zuckerberg and Jeff Bezos.

Tech workers are already rejecting this false choice and debtors must join them. From the lowest-paid cafeteria workers to privileged engineers, employees are forming unions and other associations and saying no to rampant industry sexism and anti-trans bigotry, no to using artificial intelligence to spy on vulnerable communities, no to military contracts, and no to partnerships with border patrol and the police. They are leaking information, leading walkouts, going on strike, and finding common cause.

This movement is international because the internet transcends borders, and so do the corporate goliaths it has spawned. In 2019, in advance of Uber's IPO, drivers in multiple countries went on a coordinated strike. Similarly, Amazon workers, whether they work as part of the "Mechanical Turk" program (in which people labor anonymously for pennies per task, rarely making minimum wage) or in sprawling warehouses (with their famously dangerous working conditions), are coordinating with one another and trying to build power across geographical distance. In the United States, people are successfully organizing at the local level to push back against unethical and discriminatory artificial intelligence systems. Thanks to grassroots work on the ground, facial recognition technologies have been banned outright in multiple cities in the United States, including San Francisco, California, and Somerville and Northampton, Massachusetts. The Stop LAPD Spying Coalition, an alliance that has been organizing against police surveillance in Los Angeles for years, recently forced the LAPD to abandon two predictive policing programs that led to increased police violence against working-class communities of color. In 2018, workers won a massive victory across California with the passage of AB5, which reclassifies so-called "gig workers" as employees, not independent contractors. Tech companies have pledged over $100 million to fight the law so they can continue to exploit people with impunity.

At the same time as workers and activists are fighting extractive companies, they are also trying to imagine and build alternatives. Cities across Europe are pushing for "tech sovereignty," which essentially means the right to run services and collect data to benefit local communities not American profiteers: imagine an Uber or Airbnb run by a municipality, not a multinational corporation. Meanwhile, the "platform cooperativism" movement has also been growing worldwide. There is now an international coalition pushing for alternative ways of providing goods and services, from nonprofit rideshare providers to cooperatively owned and run cellphone networks. In Oaxaca, Mexico Rhizomatica offers radically democratic, community-controlled telecommunications infrastructure. We don't need Uber or Lyft to traverse our cities, or Verizon or Comcast to connect to one another. In fact, they're an obstacle to real connection.

Fintech could be similarly transformed. Before the Coronavirus crash New York assemblyman Ron Kim, who represents a working-class district in Queens, proposed a publicly run digital payment system, something he and his colleagues describe as a "public Venmo" after the popular payment service. Kim understands that his constituents need a payment platform that doesn't charge exorbitant transaction fees, exclude people who don't have bank accounts, or violate user privacy. During the pandemic, when the government couldn't get benefits to everyone who was eligible, the need for an alternative became even more apparent. "It's even more urgent now to implement a seamless way of delivering benefits into digital wallets," Kim said.

Think about the possibilities for radically different forms of credit reporting and scoring. Right now the credit scores exist to quantify risk for lenders, and to force borrowers to conform to the dictates of creditors, employers, and landlords. But in a genuinely democratic economy, where none of us have to go into debt for any basic needs, household debt will be far less ubiquitous. Nevertheless, there would likely still be a role for extending credit and determining risks. But what kinds of risks we are looking for, and what counts as creditworthiness, could dramatically change. If credit is just a kind of trust, we need a way of determining which entities are trustworthy and which are not. The risk worth assessing in such a system would not be a risk to a lender or investor, but a risk to the community. For example, our current credit rating systems don't factor in the long-term ecological damage caused by infrastructure projects when those projects are being financed and insured. In theory, we could use machine learning technology to ensure a more holistic accounting of benefits and risks in the future.

We have to keep this in mind: the big problem isn't technology, it's the underlying political economy. The question isn't whether robots will take our jobs, but who owns the robots and who collects the rewards. In a post-capitalist world, our collective data commons could be used to radically different, socially productive ends. For example, it could help guide free, carbon-neutral public transit options to serve people as swiftly as possible. Predictive analytics could be used to facilitate a democratization and socialization of the economy, instead of monopolized profits. Automation could be employed not to make workers vulnerable but to eliminate soul-destroying drudgery and free people to do more meaningful work. Artificial intelligence and machine learning could be used to help people have more autonomy on the job, instead of forcing human beings to perform more like automatons. The internet's global reach could facilitate cross-cultural exchange and internationalism, instead of high-tech neocolonialism and nationalist reaction.

Ben Tarnoff has helpfully laid out some of the principles to guide the fight over networked technology. He argues we will need to employ four different approaches to the internet, depending on what aspect is under consideration: public ownership (probably best suited for infrastructure and services of a certain scale), cooperative ownership (smaller scale enterprises would work especially well here), non-ownership (a lot of software should be free, so the information can be easily exchanged across platforms and devices and the internet can continue to evolve), and abolition (some products shouldn't exist and some data shouldn't be collected, full stop: technology employed primarily for social control or to enforce austerity should be eliminated—not "reformed" or "democratized"). As Tarnoff says, some data mines are a lot like regular mines—they just shouldn't be built. Best to keep oil in the ground and most personal data off the cloud.

Debtors have a stake in all of these fights. Technology is not something out there—it impacts every aspect of modern life. There's nothing the internet doesn't touch. The corporate intensification of data extraction and the continued erosion of hard-won labor and consumer protections as a consequence of "innovation" can only lead in one direction: more wealth for people at the top, and more debt for everyone else.

In order to change course before it's too late, we need to use all the tools at our disposal to build the world we want to see, including digital tools. We need to organize through every available channel, on the internet and off. Online spaces can be created that subvert the commercialized logic of surveillance capitalism, serving the needs of regular people, not shareholders looking to cash out. The Debt Collective is working to build a "virtual factory floor" where geographically distant debtors can meet each other so they can begin to strategize and organize together. We can also collect data as a way of addressing the massive power asymmetries we are up against. We can harvest information in a way that respects individual privacy and use it to determine patterns of exploitation, identify weak points in the system, and devise more effective tactics for fighting back.

Our present situation is unsustainable. Financial capitalism allows profits to appear out of thin air for some—those lucky enough to be part of the investor class—while the vast majority of people are driven into debt. The gains secured by a few come at tremendous cost. The value extracted comes from the earth and its inhabitants, human and nonhuman alike.

We need to create systems that are not only non-extractive but also reparative and regenerative. Regulation is a good start, but it is nowhere near enough. There has to be a revolutionary transformation of all the systems we depend on. We need an internet where data is treated as a public good, not a commodity, and our communications infrastructure is owned by all of us, not a handful of opportunists. We need a technological system where the benefits of automation are broadly shared, not hoarded by those who own the machines. We need an energy system that is distributed, community-controlled, and renewable, powered by sun, wind, and water. We need a financial system aimed at collective benefit and democratic participation, not a sociopathic one fixated on accumulation and insulating the capitalist and creditor class.

Think of all the creativity currently going to waste, of all the engineers and coders who spend their waking hours building platforms to get users to click on advertisements, or artificial intelligence to direct drones to wage war from afar. Think of all of the innovations we are denied because, while socially beneficial, they are not profitable enough for venture capitalists to support. Think of all the things we could build together if a more egalitarian economic operating system and inclusive logic drove our investments and innovations.

In order to change things, we must recognize that there is power in numbers. Not the quantification of Silicon Valley or a banker's balance sheet or the random identifier assigned by a faceless bureaucrat but the power of the many, standing in solidarity. Together, we can learn to flex that power and demand collective control of our resources, labor, data, time, technology, and lives.

CHAPTER FIVE

THE FUTURE
OF FINANCE
ECONOMIC DISOBEDIENCE
AND REPARATIVE
PUBLIC GOODS

Mass indebtedness connects those of us living in the United States with millions of others around the world—it connects Ferguson to Greece, Puerto Rico to Bolivia. These are not theoretical links but literal connections through shared institutions like Goldman Sachs, JP Morgan Chase, BlackRock, the World Bank, and the US Federal Reserve, the lender of last resort to the world. Indebtedness is a lived experience upon which solidarity can be built, and it is also a hidden geography of potential global

133

people power. Our debt is a nonviolent weapon we all have access to—if we can leverage it in concert.

Pay attention and you can see the beginnings of what has the potential to become a militant and ambitious mass debtors' movement—we need to support, strengthen, and expand the actions that many individuals are already taking. When the Coronavirus tipped the world into economic free-fall, countless people across the United States didn't pay their rent or bills because they didn't have enough money. Some did so quietly, and others went public, boldly declaring that they couldn't pay and that they shouldn't have to pay, either. *Can't pay, won't pay.*

In the early days of the pandemic, mortgage and bill collections were paused, utility shutoffs for overdue accounts were prevented, and foreclosures and evictions halted. It turns out that changing the rules that dictate our daily financial agreements is possible after all, and it can happen with remarkable speed. The challenge is ensuring that some of these changes stick and that much further reaching transformations are made. This crisis offers a chance to do more than just hit the pause button and throw a few crumbs at people in distress, resuming "business as usual" as quickly as possible. This is an opportunity to rewrite the rules so that untold millions aren't so vulnerable and exploited to begin with. To do that, we need more than protest; we need power. The debtors' revolts throughout history and around the world that we have discussed in this book offer a model we can build on. The next steps are up to us.

WE ARE ALREADY IN REVOLT

In March 2020, a small group of homeless women and children began occupying vacant homes in Los Angeles. They asserted that, as tax-paying citizens, they had a right to live in the state-owned houses rent free, especially since the Coronavirus was making life on the street even more perilous.

Soon after the pandemic began, half the US population was worried about paying rent. May 1, 2020, marked what many have called the first national rent strike, organized by local tenant groups as well as large nonprofits, demanding rent cancellation and a halt on evictions for the duration of the crisis. Anticipating the fact that millions would have trouble making their mortgages, the Trump administration preemptively paused payments for some borrowers. They did the same for most student loans.

We are likely to see more spontaneous revolts as increasing numbers of people find themselves unable to make ends meet. With tens of millions unemployed and with cities and states trying close their budget gaps by further squeezing the poor, the US may be entering a prolonged period of economic turmoil. The mass nonpayment of debts, including but not limited to housing and student loan payments, will likely become more common in the months and years to come. But in order for these actions to have maximum impact and become key leverage points in the battle against austerity and for reparative public goods, they need democratic organization—they need resources and strategic coordination to become effective over the long term. Such sustained economic disobedience campaigns can help to win deep change, including debt cancellation and essential social services, not just brief payment reprieves.

The student debt strike that the Debt Collective launched in 2015 offers a preview of what debtor organizing can accomplish. We ultimately forced the government to abolish more than $1 billion dollars (and counting) of student loan debt belonging to tens of thousands of people while also putting student debt cancellation and free college on the map. The campaign, however, is far from finished. Until we win a student debt jubilee and free public higher education for everyone, debt strikers from schools of all kinds will need to keep fighting—and we are. Our campaign has had broader implications as well. It demonstrated not only that mass debt cancellation is possible, but also that debtors organized collectively can dramatically sway public opinion. As mentioned earlier in this book, when the Debt Collective started organizing for student debt abolition and for free public college, the media called us crazy. But by 2019, multiple presidential candidates ran on those policy proposals. In early 2020 we launched an expanded strike, inviting anyone with student debt to join the movement. (Go to strike.debtcollective.org to join the strike and tell everyone you know who has student debt to do so.)

From a technical point of view, it would be incredibly easy to free this country's nearly fifty million student debtors from their loan burdens, and it would make everyone, not just those with student debt, financially better off. (All that money currently going to servicers would go to things like housing, food, and services instead, boosting the economy through a bottom-up stimulus.) All federal student debt can be erased in an instant using the authority Congress has already vested in the Department of Education. The law is called "Compromise and Settlement," and implementing it would require little more than the secretary of education's signature. But the fact that a simple mechanism exists to erase debts is not enough. It will take a movement to push public officials to actually use the authority they possess. (In fact, it took an organizing campaign to reveal that the mechanism even exists; in 2015, lawyers including Luke Herrine, an attorney and organizer with the Debt Collective, and Eileen O'Connor, then of the New York Legal Assistance Group, began researching the law's applicability to mass student loan relief.) Student debtors are currently defaulting at the rate of one million per year. Instead of suffering in isolation, they should join the Debt Collective's student debtors' union, politicizing their inability and unwillingness to pay, and demanding Compromise and Settlement be put to use.

Our guiding principle of building debtor power holds true across a range of debt types. Millions being crushed by medical debt could organize locally to demand hospitals cancel their bills or engage in a national medical debt strike to advance the cause of universal health care. Credit card debtors could rally against usurious lending practices and advocate for a socially productive, as opposed to predatory, system of credit and debt. People with debts in the criminal punishment system could organize to challenge fines and fees and other costs associated with incarceration, demanding abolition of a system that extracts on so many levels.

The possibilities for campaigns of debt resistance are practically endless. Imagine people in a small town targeting payday loan sharks, with payday debtors refusing payment until the service is eradicated from their town. Payday lenders generate a significant portion of their revenue through "alternative financial services" such as bill paying or check cashing, charging people exorbitant fees to access and use their own money. Debtors could build alliances with local labor groups on the grounds that payday loans are wage theft, with racial justice groups on the grounds that predatory lenders target people of color, and with religious groups that have a moral commitment to resisting usury. Those same payday debtors could move on to organize at the state level to push to have payday lenders banned, so that neighboring towns are no longer exploited. Then imagine a community that provides those necessary financial services free of charge as an act of mutual aid.

Imagine teachers, who are often buried in student debt, organizing along with their students for debt cancellation and free education. Imagine nurses organizing alongside their indebted patients for universal health care. Imagine borrowers acting in solidarity with striking workers. Imagine workers of all kinds refusing debts, in connection with a campaign for a federal job guarantee that promises everyone dignified, meaningful, well-paid, and ecologically sustainable work. These sorts of actions are already underway. In May 2020 a coalition of more than twenty tenant, environmental, and community groups, including the Democratic Socialists of America, united to support a "utilities strike" in which people across the state of New York refused to pay their electric and gas bills. The coalition demanded the forgiveness of all energy debts during the pandemic, a two-year moratorium

on shut-offs, and what they call "public power"—"democratically controlled, publicly owned, 100 percent renewable energy for all New Yorkers."

Debtors could play an invaluable role pushing for structural solutions to the problem of mass indebtedness. We
don't need lower interest rates or less predatory loan terms,
we need truly public, socialized finance: public control over
public money. After conducting debt audits, debtors' unions
could build coalitions that advance the demand for public
banks. North Dakota already has a public bank, so does Ger-
many, and coalitions of activists and organizations in New
York, Pennsylvania, and California are currently mobilizing
toward this goal. Debtors in the US could also push to retool
the post office as a public banking service, something offered
in many countries. A system of public banks could allow municipalities to democratically determine who receives credit,
rather than permitting private banks to pick and choose who
has access to financing and under what conditions. Such a
system could also play a role in reparative finance: prioritizing the allocation of resources to those who have historically
been excluded or the most exploited by traditional banking
services. Public banks could help cities fund production of
necessary goods and services including housing, food, clothing, health care, education, and ecologically sustainable energy systems.

CLIMATE DEFAULTERS

The battle to save the planet is another area in which organized blocs of debtors can contribute, and socialized finance can play a role there too. The reckless pursuit of profits—and the indebtedness that generates for the great majority—does not lead to prosperity but rather to a society teetering on the edge of ecological collapse. High interest rates lock us into the perpetual pursuit of growth, accelerating and intensifying the destruction of the natural world, since charging interest assumes that there will be more tomorrow than there is today. Thus our debt-fueled economy demands that land and labor and inequality between people be exploited ever more intensely. Debtors' unions could challenge this dynamic by organizing households across the country to stop making credit card or mortgage payments to banks that fund fossil fuel expansion, including JP Morgan Chase and Wells Fargo. Municipalities could also refuse to issue payments to or bank with entities in the business of planetary destruction.

Climate change, more than anything else, urgently raises the fundamental question: who owes what to whom? Environmental justice organizers have long focused on the fact that those who have done the least to cause ecological destruction often pay the steepest price, while those most responsible are shielded from the repercussions of their actions (or inactions). The notion of "climate debt" was developed by organizers in the Global South to help analyze the fundamental imbalance of this relationship, with some researchers now estimating that the United States owes developing nations more than $4 trillion for exceeding its carbon allotment.

The Global North hasn't just burned the most carbon, it has also reaped the economic benefits of fossil fuel–based capitalism. The framework of climate debt demolishes the misguided idea that wealthy countries are supplying aid to the rest of the world. As Bolivia's chief climate negotiator, Angelica Navarro, puts it, "What we are asking for is repayment. We are not asking for aid.... We want developed countries to comply with their obligation and pay their debt." The wealthy Global North owes a debt to the rest of the world, and the payment could take many forms: offering safe harbor for climate refugees, writing off the sovereign debts of the countries most ravaged by the crisis, or investing in global, sustainable, and publicly owned energy supply chains.

Building the power of debtors is critical because, as our world heats up, one danger is that we will enter an era of carbon austerity in which the rich and powerful use violence to impose carbon-use restrictions on the poor. We are already seeing signs of this, from the Yellow Vest movement in France to California, where water is being rationed in low-income communities while golf courses in wealthy areas continue to irrigate with abandon. We need to ensure that the well-heeled do not attempt to address climate change on the backs of the poor.

Financial elites and those with resources to insulate themselves from the ravages of climate change cannot be counted on to invest in a sustainable future or a democratic future. What did they do when the cost of a barrel of oil hit $0, weeks into the Coronavirus pandemic? Instead of seizing the opportunity to euthanize the fossil fuel sector and fund a transition to sustainable energy, the government offered a massive handout to keep a dying, deadly industry alive. US fossil fuel companies secured tens of millions of dollars of public money in the form of forgivable loans originally intended for struggling small businesses, free money some companies intended to use to pay off preexisting debts. Corporate interests are well organized and have secured ample state support and debt cancellation as a result. Debtors should take note.

FUNDING THE FUTURE

We deserve a society that sees health care not just as a human right but as a public good inseparable from the broader ecology—a society that understands public health must account for the air we breathe, the water we drink, the food we eat, and the land that gives us life. We deserve access to education that is not just career training but also an expansive and lifelong process of encouraging curiosity and fostering informed, critical, and creative thinking. We deserve housing that is publicly funded as a community resource, not as a speculative asset or a private commodity. We must work to create a society that can plan ahead and sustain itself over the long term, without burning through its resources so a few can profit here and now.

The distinction between a human right and a public good is crucial. It's the difference between a theoretical entitlement and a concrete good or service that you actually receive. Building on the work of anthropologist James Ferguson, we have to shift our vision from a "right to" something (a right to housing, to education, to health) to *a material share of that thing*. A house. An education. Health care. To move from human rights to material shares is to move from abstract equalities, rarely realized in practice, to the distribution of real goods to those who are their rightful owners.

As we discussed in chapter 2, the history of racist land theft and environmental destruction continues to shape our lives in the present. This is why debt abolition alone is not enough. The public goods we fight for must also *repair* the structural violence of racial capitalism and *redress* massive land dispossession from indigenous peoples. This means that a student debt strike and jubilee must aim to transform our educational system, not just make it tuition free. When we talk about free higher education—state-funded colleges and universities— we also need to talk about the so-called public land on which these universities sit, and the intergenerational wealth transfer that land represents from indigenous people to settlers. Because public land is stolen land, as indigenous activist groups such as The Red Nation remind us, then re-commoning that land must be part of the process of redress. When we advocate for *free* higher education, we also have to talk about *freedom*. During the 2020 uprisings, for example, UCLA allowed the Los Angeles Police Department to turn the university's Jackie

Robinson Stadium into a field for arresting and detaining protesters. Simply ending tuition is not enough to make higher education truly liberated or liberating if colleges and universities are not true sanctuaries from police violence. Or, take the example of public health care. Medical disparities are also racial disparities. Precisely because of the racialized nature of capitalism, Black and Latinx communities disproportionately belong to the workforce deemed "essential" during the coronavirus pandemic yet left uninsured. These workers are not only more exposed to the virus but are also more likely to die from it or to suffer a more severe infection, due to preexisting conditions—the cumulative result of decades of health care discrimination in a privately financed system that prioritizes profit. Thus, any public medical care that we enact after a medical debt jubilee will have to be *reparative* medical care, working with community health networks and other providers to affirmatively eliminate racial differentiation in health outcomes and overall wellness.

The money is there for these policies and much more. It belongs to us, the public. The federal budget, it's important to note, is not like a household budget. The US government doesn't have to have the money in advance (by raising it through taxes, for example) because it is the issuer of the US dollar. This means that, as a nation, we are not financially constrained in the way households are, or in the way some other countries are. While federal spending has to be managed and dollars have to be spent in ways that the economy can absorb, US government debt (known as the deficit) is actually sustainable, unlike our personal debt, which is not. The United States can't go broke. Individuals can. Instead of fearing deficits across the board, we need to ask what they are for. Was the debt incurred to steal from the public or invest in the future?

Could the Department of Education wipe student loan debts off the books? Absolutely. Could Congress vote to cover the cost of free public colleges and universities? Of course. After all, it could conjure up trillions of dollars for corporate bailouts in 2008 and again in 2020, when a massive spending package to rescue cruise lines, hotels, airlines, and even private equity firms passed without any corresponding cuts or tax hikes. We don't need to tax the rich first or borrow their money. (As the economist Stephanie Kelton has noted, "Bonds are a gift to investors, not a sign of dependency on them.") In the United States, the challenge isn't finding the money, it's ensuring that it goes to the things we need. We're in a power struggle over spending, not a struggle to raise funds.

Of course, that's not what politicians tell us. They go on and on about how we can't afford public services and obsess over the national debt. Such an appeal to budget considerations, when weighing a potential piece of legislation, is known in Congress as a "pay for"—where you have to announce how you will pay for a program, either by reducing costs or raising other revenue, before you implement it. In reality, it's just a way to refuse to spend public money on the things the public needs. Republicans love to brand themselves as deficit hawks while bloating the military budget, slashing taxes, and bailing out failing industries. In 2019, for example, the US Congress authorized a $738 billion annual military budget, $38 billion *more* than the military requested. (As Kelton has pointed out, there was no debate about this budget authorization. "What you have to find is *the votes* [in Congress]. You don't have to find the money," she said. If the votes are there, the money will be too.) Democrats, meanwhile, are even more beholden to the question, "How will you pay for it?" than their ostensible adversaries. Consider Joe Biden, who, in the midst of a pandemic, was asked whether, as president, he would sign Medicare for All legislation if it landed on his desk. His answer was no. He would veto such a bill because of the high costs supposedly attached to universal health care. Ideology, not economics, is why we will likely see the federal government imposing austerity measures in the coming months and years. Having spent trillions of dollars on corporations, they will tell the rest of us that there is nothing left. Debtors' unions need to push back against this obfuscation, emboldened by the fact our debt payments represent income streams for some of the same people who eagerly support state budget cuts, but only after the government has added to the so-called national debt to cover their losses. They don't deserve any more of our money.

When it comes to global finance, the United States is in an extremely privileged position. Countries around the world have different degrees of what is called "monetary sovereignty"— varying levels of power and authority over their own currencies. (Remember Greece? Giving theirs up was a condition of joining the European Union.) That means not every country can deficit spend on public goods. No country in the world right now has the monetary sovereignty that the US has, in part because many countries also borrow in US dollars, a fact that stems in part from the histories of US imperialism we discussed earlier. In addition, every day the Federal Reserve makes important decisions about how to allocate private capital around the world. This means that US foreign policy, energy policy, and the US extraction of resources abroad not only come with guns, but they also require everyone else to depend on the dollar as a form of global enforcement.

As a result, the Federal Reserve wields an enormous amount of power, domestically and internationally. If our vision of reparative public goods is transnational, and contests the colonial and imperial geography of borders, we will have to reimagine how this system can be made to work for ordinary people around the globe, as well as for future generations. In a truly equitable future of finance, all investment priorities would be set by the public instead of a small handful of elites. There is a centralized planning process already in place between the Federal Reserve, big banks, and securities dealers, it is just not democratically accountable or publicly shared. Money allocation is a political process, not a result of some invisible hand, which means we can and should take democratic control over it. "The challenge now," economist J. W. Mason writes, "is to politicize central banks—to make them the object of public debate and popular pressure."

A democratically controlled monetary system could help advance an environmental agenda by opening up new ways to fund a green transition. Imagine if the trillions of dollars in economic stimulus shoveled at corporations at the onset of the pandemic had been used instead to fund a Green New Deal. Governments could issue bonds at both local and national levels to be spent exclusively on green projects—moving away from fossil fuels, creating good jobs, supporting research and development in renewable technologies, and more. Such funds could also be used to advance labor market inclusion policies, prioritizing the employment of people with criminal records, for example, or others who have historically suffered from labor market discrimination. Law professor Saule Omarova has proposed what she calls a "national investment authority" that would function like an asset manager, owned and managed by the public. Massive pools of collective money that already exist in pension funds or insurance companies would provide much of the investment here. The aforementioned public banks would be useful to facilitate this process as well. They could assure that investment instruments like bonds are no longer brokered through for-profit banks but through publicly managed financial institutions.

There are lots of ways to restructure our economy to benefit the poor and the working class. The limit is real resources, not financial resources. To fund Medicare for All, College for All, or a Green New Deal, we don't need to ask if we have the money. All we have to ask is, do we have the doctors? The nurses? The professors? The classrooms? Do we have people who can get to work building a more sustainable society? Do we have the real resources to deliver on the policies? There have to be people who can be hired and paid to teach, to deliver medical care, and to build high-speed low-carbon transit systems, and there have to be companies ready to manufacture the stethoscopes, textbooks, and train carriages. In the transition to a green economy, carbon budgets and other ecological limits must be prioritized, but we still have a great deal of flexibility when it comes to financial resources, a radical potential we have yet to tap.

BUILDING REAL POWER

We have already noted that redress and repair are central concepts to a new vision of public goods. The Movement for Black Lives and The Red Nation, for example, have both written policy proposals for reparative public goods. We also take inspiration from the Freedom Budget, which was co-written by the civil rights activist A. Philip Randolph and published in 1966. The Freedom Budget proposed robust federal funding for a job guarantee, universal health care, a basic income, and a clean environment for all. After the passage of the Voting Rights Act, organizers began to question whether it made sense to continue to refer to their struggle as a "civil rights movement" without paying deeper attention to the distribution of wealth and ownership in society. As the socialist and activist Bayard Rustin put it, advancing the struggle for Black equality required "a refashioning of our political economy." Today's activists are already taking up the call. In 2020, in response to Los Angeles mayor Eric Garcetti's austerity budget that slashed everything but the police, a coalition produced The People's Budget. It demanded funding for public services, not cops. We need to address the root causes of inequality by investing in schools, housing, meaningful work, and more. As the writer Jamelle Bouie recently put it, "The fight for equal personhood can't help but also be a struggle for economic justice."

At the same time that we look to these historical and contemporary examples for inspiration, we are mindful of Professor Keeanga Yamahtta-Taylor's warning. "Sometimes it is necessary to imagine what freedom might look like," she wrote, "but after demands have been delivered and promises have been made, someone has got to fight to make them a reality." Our proposals need to be backed up by real power, or they will remain just that—proposals.

Building power means organizing to win material gains for the greatest number of people while never losing sight of racial capitalism's disproportionate harms. Spontaneous revolt or outbursts of dissent can only begin to transform our economy. Effective protest and insurgencies that have an impact are the result of strategic thinking, trial and error, relationship building, and the development of organizational structures that allow large numbers of people to smoothly join movements and take up meaningful roles within them. Ensuring that such organizations are antiracist, anti-patriarchal, and anti-ableist is part of a critical and ongoing process. That work includes supporting existing institutions such as labor unions, mutual aid efforts, environmental justice groups, and abolition organizations while building new institutional forms—including debtors' unions. "Solidarity is something that is made and remade and remade. It never just is," the abolitionist scholar Ruth Wilson Gilmore has said. We must advance this difficult undertaking or risk becoming a marginal tendency when we need to build a mass movement.

As the organizer and writer Jane McKelvey often says, there are "no shortcuts" in organizing. It takes collective intelligence and imagination as well as time and resources. Those who are the most oppressed cannot be expected to sustain organizing efforts without resources. This is one "pay for" that actually matters: organizers should be paid a living wage, just like anyone else who performs socially useful labor, and effective mobilizations often require a budget. Social movements, especially those that consider themselves leftist, must get more serious about money and about how the *work* of changing the world will be funded. We have to ask whether current models for getting resources to organizations and movement participants are up to the task. For example, there are many important critiques of the "nonprofit industrial complex" and of the fact that large foundations and individual philanthropists have historically funneled resources in ways that clip activists' wings and blunt our demands. Organizations that aim to be both sustainable and accountable to the working class should aim to rely on dues-paying members, not wealthy donors.

Getting serious about building power means bringing as many people as possible into the process of social transformation. Building a mass base, in turn, means working across existing race and class formations. As we've tried to show, the way debt operates at the municipal, national, and international levels makes it an issue that affects us all—even those who are fortunate enough to personally be debt free. At the same time, while change is often led from below, we cannot simply leave the enormous struggle ahead to those who are most exploited and impoverished. What is the role of the professional class and of relatively affluent people in the fight for the future? How can their privileges be best put to use? Few are safe in today's precarious, debt-fueled economy, and the majority of people, including those who are part of the increasingly downwardly mobile "middle class," have far more to gain from struggles for social change than they have to lose.

It is time to expand our imaginations of what's possible, moving beyond idealizations of a welfare state to what we might call a *solidarity state*—a state that not only redistributes resources to "beneficiaries" but also democratizes control over how those resources are produced, allocated, and managed. These values must also inform our organizing work. Regular people understand better than many so-called experts how they are exploited and what it would take to be truly free. The task is to build democratic institutions that can open space for all of us to learn and think, develop new ideas and proposals, and strategize about how to implement them. It is a process that demands shared leadership and decision making. The word *credit*, as we've said, originally meant trust. Trust is one form of credit that should be more widely extended.

REPOSSESSING WHAT'S OURS

A debt is an attempt to put a number on something that is often unquantifiable. How could we possibly put a number on what we owe to our ancestors? How could we put a limit on the value of someone's life? What is the future worth? When we sign loan contracts and dutifully pay our debts month after month, we are not just giving our lives to the 1 percent; we are also handing over our futures, something creditors have no right to. Since our obligations to one another are infinite, putting price tags on them is an act of violence. We need to cultivate and support popular movements that can collectively stop cooperating with those entities that, by dictating the terms on which we access wages, housing, health care, education, and more, exercise increasing control over our fates.

We see indebtedness as a bond that ties us together across borders, and we must use those bonds to push for a new social contract—indeed, that is what solidarity means. Can we honor the connections we have to one another, including to those in other parts of the world? Are you willing to fight for someone you don't know? These questions can seem like moral appeals intended to move people of good conscience, but we actually mean them in a much more literal and practical way. What we are facing is not a crisis of conscience or of good judgment. Instead, we are facing an unprecedented economic emergency rooted in centuries of racist, colonialist, and capitalist exploitation and intensified by decades of rapacious financialization and new technologies of extraction. People know something is wrong: most people want wealth redistribution, public services, and a chance to live in dignity. This means the battle ahead isn't primarily about changing hearts and minds. It's a struggle to change social structures. It is a struggle for socialism, for collective power over the world in which we live and for a political and economic system based on the transformative principles of care and repair.

The time has come to default on the powerful so we can finally honor our true debts to one another. Through strategic campaigns of economic disobedience and debt refusal, we can help repair past damage, rescue our planet, and repossess our lives. By resisting together, we reclaim all that has been stolen. Alone, our debts are a burden; together they can make us powerful. We owe it to one another to fight back.

FURTHER READING

Patricia Adams, *Odious Debts: Loose Lending, Corruption, and the Third World's Environmental Legacy* (Earthscan, 1991).

Kate Aronoff, Alyssa Battistoni, Daniel Aldana Cohen, and Thea Riofrancos, *A Planet to Win: Why We Need a Green New Deal* (Verso, 2019).

Mehrsa Baradaran, *The Color of Money: Black Banks and the Racial Wealth Gap* (Belknap Press, 2017).

Sven Beckert, *Empire of Cotton: A Global History* (Knopf, 2014).

David Blacker, *The Falling Rate of Learning and the Neoliberal Endgame* (Zero Books, 2013).

Grace Blakeley, *Stolen: How to Save the World from Financialisation* (Repeater Books, 2019).

Mark Blyth, *Austerity: The History of a Dangerous Idea* (Oxford University Press, 2013).

Ellen Hodgson Brown, *Web of Debt: The Shocking Truth about Our Money System and How We Can Break Free* (Third Millennium Press, 2008).

Lendol Calder, *Financing the American Dream: A Cultural History of Consumer Credit* (Princeton University Press, 2001).

Alan Collinge, *The Student Loan Scam: The Most Oppressive Debt in U.S. History and How We Can Fight Back* (Beacon, 2010).

Melinda Cooper, *Family Values: Between Neoliberalism and the New Social Conservatism* (Zone Books, 2017).

Tressie McMillan Cottom, *Lower Ed: The Troubling Rise of For-Profit Colleges in the New Economy* (The New Press, 2017).

William A. Darity Jr. and A. Kirsten Mullen, *From Here to Equality: Reparations for Black Americans in the Twenty-First Century* (University of North Carolina Press, 2020).

David Dayen, *Chain of Title: How Three Ordinary Americans Uncovered Wall Street's Great Foreclosure Fraud* (The New Press, 2016).

Jeremy Dear, Paula Dear, and Tim Jones, *Life and Debt: Global Studies of Debt and Resistance* (Jubilee Debt Campaign, 2013).

Richard Dienst, *The Bonds of Debt: Borrowing Against the Common Good* (Verso, 2011).

Tamara Draut, *Strapped: Why America's 20- and 30-Somethings Can't Get Ahead* (Doubleday, 2006).

Charles Duhigg, "What Does Your Credit Card Company Know About You?" *New York Times*, May 12, 2009.

Enric Duran, "I Have 'Robbed' 492,000 Euros Whom Most Rob Us in Order to Denounce Them and Build Some Alternatives Society," enricduran.cat, 2015, https://enricduran.cat/en/i-have-robbed-492000-euros-whom-most-rob-us-order-denounce-them-and-build-some-alternatives-society-0/.

Nick Estes, *Our History Is the Future: Standing Rock Versus the Dakota Access Pipeline, and the Long Tradition of Indigenous Resistance* (Verso, 2019).

Jonathan Franklin, "Chile's Students' Debts Go Up in Smoke," *Guardian*, May 23, 2014, https://www.theguardian.com/world/2014/may/23/chile-student-loan-debts-fried-potatoes#.

Charles Geisst, *Beggar Thy Neighbor: A History of Usury and Debt* (University of Pennsylvania Press, 2013).

Ruth Wilson Gilmore, *Golden Gulag: Prisons, Surplus, Crisis, and Opposition in Globalizing California* (University of California Press, 2007).

David Graeber, *Debt: The First 5,000 Years* (Melville House, 2011).

Darrick Hamilton and William A. Darity Jr., "The Political Economy of Education, Financial Literacy, and the Racial Wealth Gap," Federal Reserve Bank of St. Louis *Review* 99, no. 1 (First Quarter 2017):59–76, http://

dx.doi.org/10.20955/r.2017.59-76.

Cheryl Harris, "Whiteness as Property," *Harvard Law Review* 106, no. 8 (June 1993):1707–1791.

Saidiya Hartman, "Fashioning Obligation: Indebted Servitude and the Fetters of Slavery" in *Scenes of Subjection: Terror, Slavery and Self-Making in Nineteenth-Century America* (Oxford University Press, 1997).

David Harvey, *A Brief History of Neoliberalism* (Oxford University Press, 2007).

Michael Hudson, *The Bubble and Beyond: The Road from Industrial Capitalism to Finance Capitalism and Debt Peonage* (Islet, 2012).

C. L. R. James, *The Black Jacobins: Toussaint L'Ouverture and the San Domingo Revolution* (Vintage, 1989).

Cryn Johannsen, *Solving the Student Loan Crisis: Dreams, Diplomas & A Lifetime Debt* (New Insights Press, 2016).

Howard Karger, *Shortchanged: Life and Debt in the Fringe Economy* (Berrett-Koehler, 2005).

Stephanie Kelton, *The Deficit Myth: Modern Monetary Theory and the Birth of the People's Economy* (Public Affairs, 2020).

Stephanie Kelton, Catherine Ruetschlin, and Marshall Steinbaum, *The Macroeconomic Effects of Student Debt Cancellation* (Levy Economics Institute, 2018), http://www.levyinstitute.org/publications/

the-macroeconomic-effects-of-student-debt-cancellation.

Naomi Klein, *The Battle for Paradise: Puerto Rico Takes on the Disaster Capitalists* (Haymarket Books, 2018).

Greta Krippner, *Capitalizing on Crisis: The Political Origins of the Rise of Finance* (Harvard University Press, 2011).

Robert Kuttner, *Debtors' Prison: The Politics of Austerity Versus Possibility* (Knopf, 2013).

John Lanchester, *I.O.U.: Why Everyone Owes Everyone and No One Can Pay* (Simon and Schuster, 2010).

James MacDonald, *A Free Nation Deep in Debt: The Financial Roots of Democracy* (Farrar, Straus, and Giroux, 2003).

Robert Manning, *Credit Card Nation: The Consequences of America's Addiction to Credit Cards* (Basic Books, 2000).

Bill McKibben, "Money Is the Oxygen on Which the Fire of Global Warming Burns," *New Yorker*, September 17, 2019, https://www.newyorker.com/news/daily-comment/money-is-the-oxygen-on-which-the-fire-of-global-warming-burns.

Jesse Meyerson, "How to Get Rid of Your Landlord and Socialize American Housing, in 3 Easy Steps," *Nation*, December 8, 2015, https://www.thenation.com/article/archive/how-to-get-rid-of-your-landlord-and-socialize-american-housing-in-3-easy-steps/.

The Movement for Black Lives Policy Platforms, https://m4bl.org/policy-platforms/.

Mujeres Creando, "The Feminism of the Streets" *Do or Die*, no. 10 (2003): 173–77, http://www.doordie.org.uk/ issues/issue-10/25-mujeres-creando.html.

Donna Murch, "Paying for Punishment: The New Debtors' Prison," *Boston Review*, August 1, 2016, http://bostonreview.net/editors-picks-us/ donna-murch-paying-punishment.

K-Sue Park, "Money, Mortgages, and the Conquest of America," *Law and Social Inquiry* 41, no. 4 (Fall 2016): 1006–1035.

Cheryl Payer, *The Debt Trap: The International Monetary Fund and the Third World* (Monthly Review Press, 1974).

Ross Perlin, *Intern Nation: How to Earn Nothing and Learn Little in the Brave New Economy* (Verso, 2011).

Thomas Piketty, *Capital in the Twenty-First Century* (Harvard University Press, 2014).

The Red Nation, "The Red Deal: Indigenous Action to Save Our Earth," https://therednation.org/2019/09/22/ the-red-deal/.

Gary Rivlin, *Broke, USA: From Pawnshops to Poverty, Inc.— How the Working Poor Became Big Business* (Harper Business, 2010).

Cedric Robinson, *Black Marxism: The Making of the Black Radical Tradition* (University of North Carolina Press, 2000).

Andrew Ross, *Creditocracy and the Case for Debt Refusal* (O/R Books, 2014).

Robert Samuels, *Why Public Higher Education Should Be Free: How to Decrease Cost and Increase Quality at American Universities* (Rutgers University Press, 2013).

Thomas Sankara, "A United Front Against Debt," speech, July 29, 1987, delivered at the 1987 Organisation of African Unity conference, Addis Ababa, Ethiopia, https://www.viewpointmag.com/2018/02/01/united-front-debt-1987/.

Andrew Simms, Aubrey Meyer, and Nick Robbins, *Who Owes Who?: Climate Change, Debt, Equity and Survival* (Christian Aid, 1999).

Strike Debt, *The Debt Resisters' Operations Manual* (PM Press, 2014).

Keeanga-Yamahtta Taylor, *Race for Profit: How Banks and the Real Estate Industry Undermined Black Homeownership* (University of North Carolina Press, 2019).

Eric Toussaint, *The Debt System* (Haymarket Books, 2019).

Eric Toussaint and Damien Millet, *Debt, the IMF, and the World Bank; Sixty Questions, Sixty Answers* (Monthly Review Press, 2010).

Jackie Wang, *Carceral Capitalism* (Semiotext(e)/Intervention, 2018).

Brett Williams, *Debt for Sale: A Social History of the Credit Trap* (University of Pennsylvania Press, 2004).

Eric Williams, *Capitalism and Slavery* (University of North Carolina Press, 1994).

Jeff Williams, "Student Debt and The Spirit of Indenture," *Dissent*, Fall 2008, https://www.dissentmagazine.org/article/student-debt-and-the-spirit-of-indenture.

ABOUT THE AUTHORS

THE DEBT COLLECTIVE is a new kind of union—a debtors' union—that transforms individual financial struggles into a source of collective power by enabling its members to engage in strategic campaigns of economic disobedience and debt refusal. The Debt Collective's writers' bloc includes Ann Larson, Astra Taylor, Hannah Appel, Thomas Gokey, and Laura Hanna.

ASTRA TAYLOR is a filmmaker, author, and activist. She is the author of *The People's Platform: Taking Back Power and Culture in the Digital Age* and *Democracy May Not Exist, But We'll Miss It When It's Gone.*

ABOUT
HAYMARKET BOOKS

HAYMARKET BOOKS is a radical, independent, non-profit book publisher based in Chicago. Our mission is to publish books that contribute to struggles for social and economic justice. We strive to make our books a vibrant and organic part of social movements and the education and development of a critical, engaged, international left.

We take inspiration and courage from our namesakes, the Haymarket martyrs, who gave their lives fighting for a better world. Their 1886 struggle for the eight-hour day—which gave us May Day, the international workers' holiday—reminds workers around the world that ordinary people can organize and struggle for their own liberation. These struggles continue today across the globe—struggles against oppression, exploitation, poverty, and war.

Since our founding in 2001, Haymarket Books has published more than five hundred titles. Radically independent, we seek to drive a wedge into the risk-averse world of corporate book publishing.

Our authors include Noam Chomsky, Arundhati Roy, Rebecca Solnit, Angela Y. Davis, Howard Zinn, Amy Goodman, Wallace Shawn, Mike Davis, Winona LaDuke, Ilan Pappé, Richard Wolff, Dave Zirin, Keeanga-Yamahtta Taylor, Nick Turse, Dahr Jamail, David Barsamian, Elizabeth Laird, Amira Hass, Mark Steel, Avi Lewis, Naomi Klein, and Neil Davidson. We are also the trade publishers of the acclaimed Historical Materialism Book Series and of Dispatch Books.